Mute Vol 2 #7

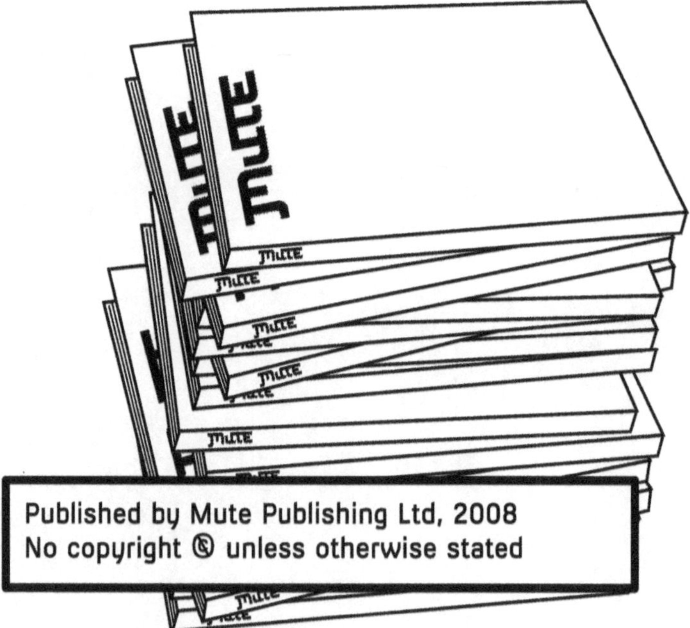

Mute
Mute
Mute
Mute
Mute
Mute
Mute
Mute
Mute

EDITOR
Josephine Berry Slater <josie@metamute.org>

DEPUTY EDITOR
Benedict Seymour <ben@metamute.org>

ASSISTANT EDITOR
Anthony Iles <anthony@metamute.org>

EDITORIAL BOARD
Josephine Berry Slater, Matthew Hyland
<infuriant@autistici.org>, Anthony Iles, Demetra
Kotouza <demetra@inventati.org>, Hari Kunzru
<hari@metamute.org>, Pauline van Mourik
Broekman, Benedict Seymour, Laura Sullivan
<alchemical44@yahoo.co.uk> and
Simon Worthington

MUTE PUBLISHING ADVISORY BOARD
Ceri Hand, Sally Jane Norman, Andy Wilson,
Sukhdev Sandhu

PUBLISHERS
Pauline van Mourik Broekman
<pauline@metamute.org>
Simon Worthington <simon@metamute.org>

ISSUE DESIGN
Simon Worthington, Giorgio Agostoni
<g.agostoni@gmail.com> and OSP
http://ospublishing.constantvzw.org
Designed using 100% FLOSS tools, thanks to:
ScriBus, Gimp, Inkscape, FontForge and
OpenOffice.

ADVERTISING & MARKETING
Lois Olmstead <lois@metamute.org>

WEBSITE
Metamute.org is powered by Drupal and
CiviCRM FLOSS Software, with additional
software services by our very own OpenMute
http://openmute.org

TECH SUPPORT
Website upgrade: Greenman at Code+
Web infrastructure: Darron Broad
<darron@kewl.org>

INTERNS
Special thanks to: Stefano di Cicco, Lars Dittmer,
Jaya Klara Brekke

ADMINISTRATOR
Sam Gul <sam@metamute.org>

COVER
Concept: Anthony, Ben and Josie; realisation:
Giorgio Agostoni, Simon Worthington

DRYPOINT ILLUSTRATIONS IN THIS ISSUE
Lee Galpin <galpinl@aol.com>

OFFICE
Mute, Unit 9, The Whitechapel Centre,
85 Myrdle Street, London E1 1HQ, UK
T: +44 (0)20 7377 6949
F: +44 (0)20 7377 9520
email: <mute@metamute.org>

SUBSCRIPTIONS
Sam Gul
T: +44 (0)20 7377 6949
F: +44 (0)20 7377 9520
email: <subs@metamute.org>
web: http://www.metamute.org/subs/

DISTRIBUTION UK
Central Books, 99 Wallis Road, London, E4 5LN
T: +44 (0)20 8986 4854
F: +44 (0)20 8533 5821

DISTRIBUTION US
Publishers Distribution Group Inc., 699
Washington Street, Suite 2B, Hackettstown,
NJ, 07840, USA
T: 001 (908) 813-8511
F: 001 (908) 813-8512

CONTRIBUTING
Mute welcomes contributions of all kinds. Email
<mute@metamute.org> with your ideas

You can also publish on Mute's website
[http://metamute.org]. Post news, texts, events
and comments, or upload media to the Mute
Public Library: http://pl.metamute.org

The views expressed in Mute and Metamute
are not necessarily those of the publishers or
service providers Mute is published in the UK
by Mute Publishing Ltd. and printed by
OpenMute http://openmute.org print on
demand (POD) book services in the USA and UK

Special thanks to Lee Galpin for besting every
commission we threw at him and to Beth and
Karen at Bethlem Gallery for introducing us to
his work. As ever, thanks to Laura Oldenbourg
for lending her superheroine powers

ISSN 1356-7748 - 261
ISBN 978-1-906496-07-4

Mute is supported by
The Arts Council of England

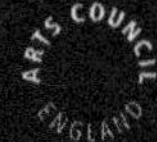

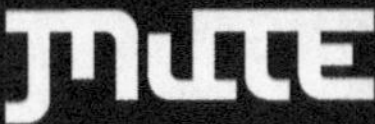

TABLE OF CONTENTS

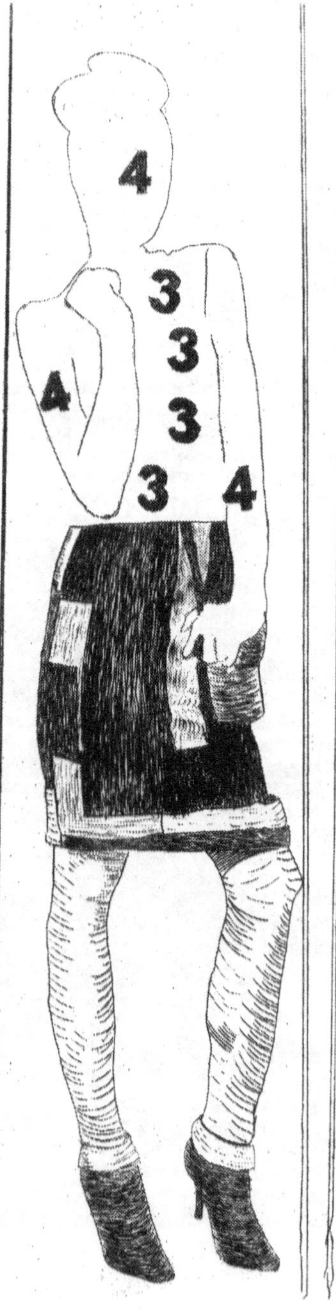

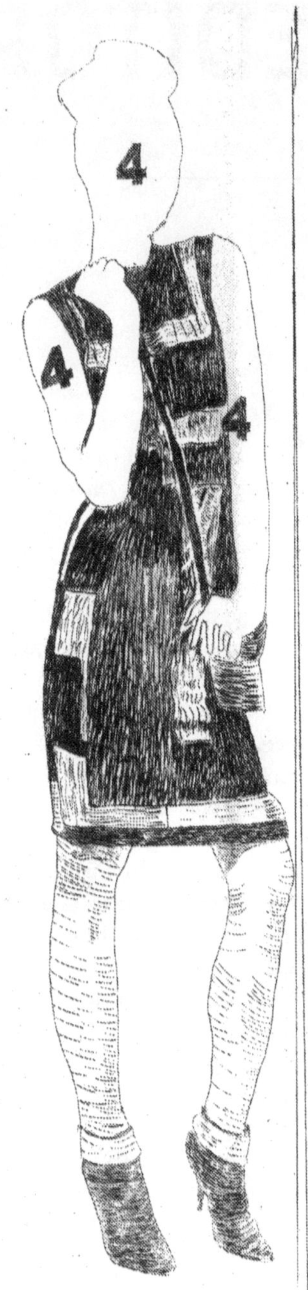

EDITORIAL

We are standing on the brink of an immense revelation. The revelation of people to states. In the UK – the surveillance workshop of the world – people are becoming increasingly visible through IT projects like the Electronic Patients Record and the National Identity Register, as well as a forthcoming points-based immigration regime premised on the ability to identify subjects and then track and cross-reference their data as never before. Joining-up data, and hence governance, is the name of the game. What are the implications then of this dangerous regime of identity capture, assessment, and tracking for political demands for representation and rights? What are the risks and advantages of visibility, of joining the demos, when identification by the state triggers joined-up 'knowledge', often with punitive results?

The bright light of IT in the hands of increasingly authoritarian regimes is chasing away the shadows that once provided the minimum of protection, income and manoeuvrability to people at the edges of society. The basic survival of the poor, undocumented or 'illegalised' often depends on the ability to operate without detection, the necessity of ID, or the creation of official records. This grey zone of anonymity is constantly squeezed in the interests of population management, border enforcement, welfare clamp-downs, technocratic convenience and, of course, the economy. This issue of Mute focuses on the exposure of subjects not just to state surveillance and databasing, but to sovereign state power enacted either through the ordinary rule of law or through its suspension in the state of emergency.

As Elizabeth Povinelli writes in these pages, 'The state of exception and its tethering to moral panic, is a routinised form of state action.' State/media orchestrated panics, usually presenting a society on the brink of calamity, have become the precondition of the state's operations. In order to justify massive social change such as 'managed migration', in which would-be immigrants to the UK will be subjected to an inhuman assessment based on 'skills', the emotive bomb of 'swamping' is detonated again and again. In order to roll back hard-won indigenous rights and 'neoliberate' communities and their lands in Australia, the bomb of culturally ingrained child sexual abuse amongst Aboriginals is detonated. As Povinelli says, these moral panics are like screaming fire in a movie theatre – no time to think, just act. The time of the here and now privileges those with power, after all, this is the time-frame in which the world's traders make fortunes.

Threats of bird flu, paedophilia, swamping, terrorism or inefficient hospital treatment are enough to convince parliaments that uncontrolled movement, indeed the chaos of life itself, must be managed. Here, blind panic combines with sober technocratic procedure: personal details must be taken and collated. As Camille Barbagallo & Nic Beuret argue in this issue, biopolitical control is achieved through the regime of rights, the 'inscription of life into the state'. This production of a national body, protected by rights, requires an outside to give it meaning, but one which is constantly under attack. Although the attainment of rights often represents the culmination of struggles to redefine the composition of this national body, to admit those people or freedoms previously excluded, it always entails life's re-inscription into the state – as well as the renewed exclusion of others.

The Strangers into Citizens campaign, that calls for an amnesty for illegal immigrants in the UK, throws up just this problem. As the campaigners explain, those granted asylum would enter a probationary period in which they would demonstrate their right to join British society as hard-working, family oriented, model citizens. Clearly then there is no universal basis for rights in the sheer fact of being human. In a series of interviews, Jaya Klara Brekke investigates how migration activists and other groups attempt to improve migrants' conditions with or without recourse to rights and asks how, in their different and often conflicting ways, they deal with the problem of 'organising in the dark'. Perhaps it is enough to venture, in response to the cover's question 'Show Invisibles?', that visibility is not only achievable through inscription in the state. Organising in the dark can of course result in other kinds of revelation such as the mass withdrawal of il/legal labour seen in the US last year during 'A Day Without Immigrants' – in this case the power of the 'invisible' was made palpably evident.

Josephine Berry Slater
<josie@metamute.org>

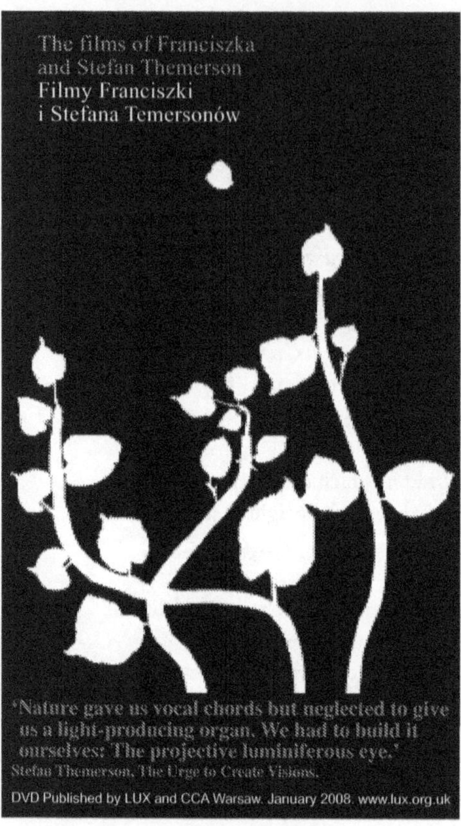

The films of Franciszka
and Stefan Themerson
Filmy Franciszki
i Stefana Temersonów
'Nature gave us vocal chords but neglected to give
us a light-producing organ. We had to build it
ourselves: The projective luminiferous eye.'
Stefan Themerson, The Urge to Create Visions.
DVD Published by LUX and CCA Warsaw. January 2008. www.lux.org.uk

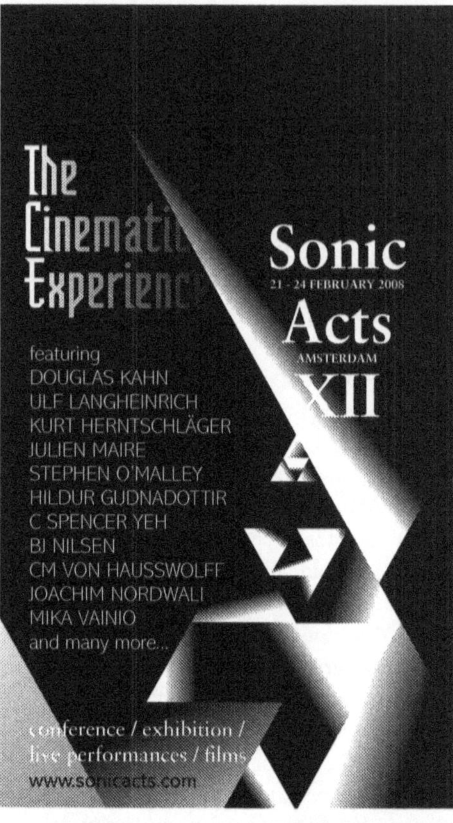

The
Cinematic
Experience
Sonic
21 - 24 FEBRUARY 2008
Acts
AMSTERDAM
XII
featuring
DOUGLAS KAHN
ULF LANGHEINRICH
KURT HERNTSCHLÄGER
JULIEN MAIRE
STEPHEN O'MALLEY
HILDUR GUDNADOTTIR
C SPENCER YEH
BJ NILSEN
CM VON HAUSSWOLFF
JOACHIM NORDWALL
MIKA VAINIO
and many more...
conference / exhibition /
live performances / films
www.sonicacts.com

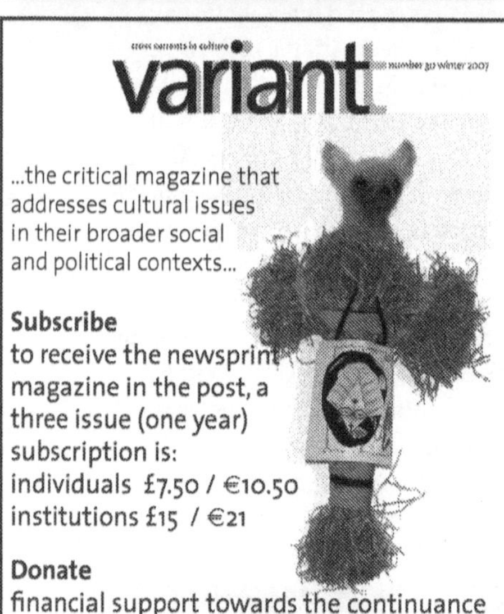

cross currents in culture
variant
number 30 winter 2007
...the critical magazine that
addresses cultural issues
in their broader social
and political contexts...

Subscribe
to receive the newsprint
magazine in the post, a
three issue (one year)
subscription is:
individuals £7.50 / €10.50
institutions £15 / €21

Donate
financial support towards the continuance
of Variant is very much appreciated

Advertise
15,000 copies are freely distributed
each issue with the help of over 420
arts, cultural, and educational spaces
throughout the UK & Ireland

www.variant.org.uk

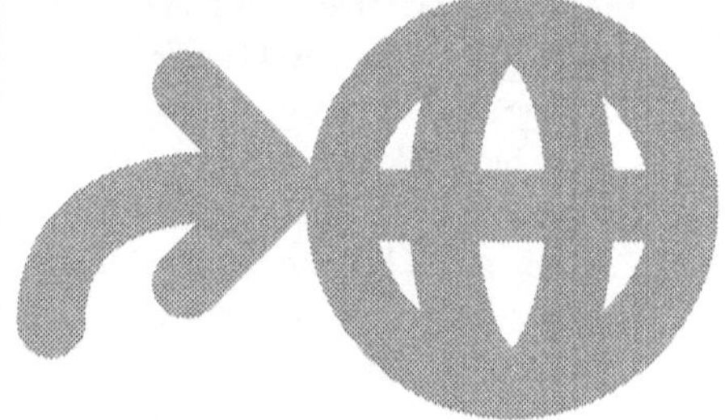

collaborate
One website, 48 countries,
5 languages. It's never been
easier to know about everything
that's happening across Europe
with arts and culture. Find ideas,
find people, find money, find
events, find debates:

www.labforculture.org

pod

Print on demand from OpenMute

OpenMute POD allows you to print books in numbers from 1 to 100+ at a fixed price of just £1.99. Compared to conventional printing, the set up fees are small too, and instead of financing your whole run in one go, POD allows you to pay as you print.

POD is a professional digital printing method that offers high quality black and white print bound with colour covers. It has existed in the corporate sector, at a high price, but only combined with new web services has it become accessible and affordable to the public. Managed through an online account, POD takes all the headache out of print setup and delivery. It makes sales and distribution simpler, too.

Drawing on our expertise in web and print publishing, OpenMute offers a full range of services at budget prices to help you make your POD book.

OpenMute services include:

* **Document preparation and delivery to the POD printer**

* **Customer online ordering and delivery service**

* **Integration into an existing web site**

* **Amazon / Paypal integration**

* **Consultancy and training**

If you'd like to talk more, get an information and pricing sheet or a free quote, then please get in touch, **<services@metamute.org>**

OpenMute POD info, http://openmute.org/

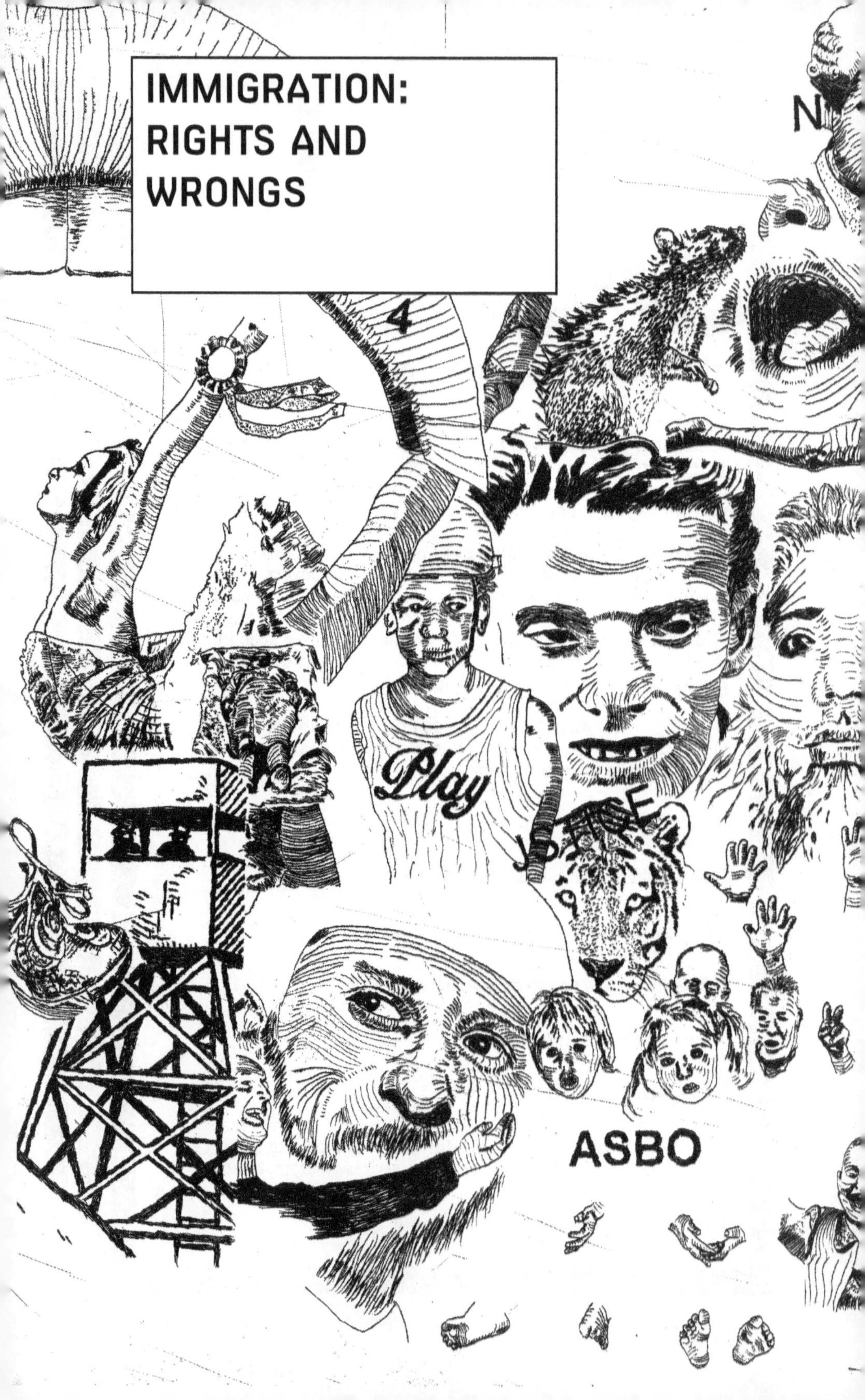

IMMIGRATION:
RIGHTS AND
WRONGS
Play
ASBO

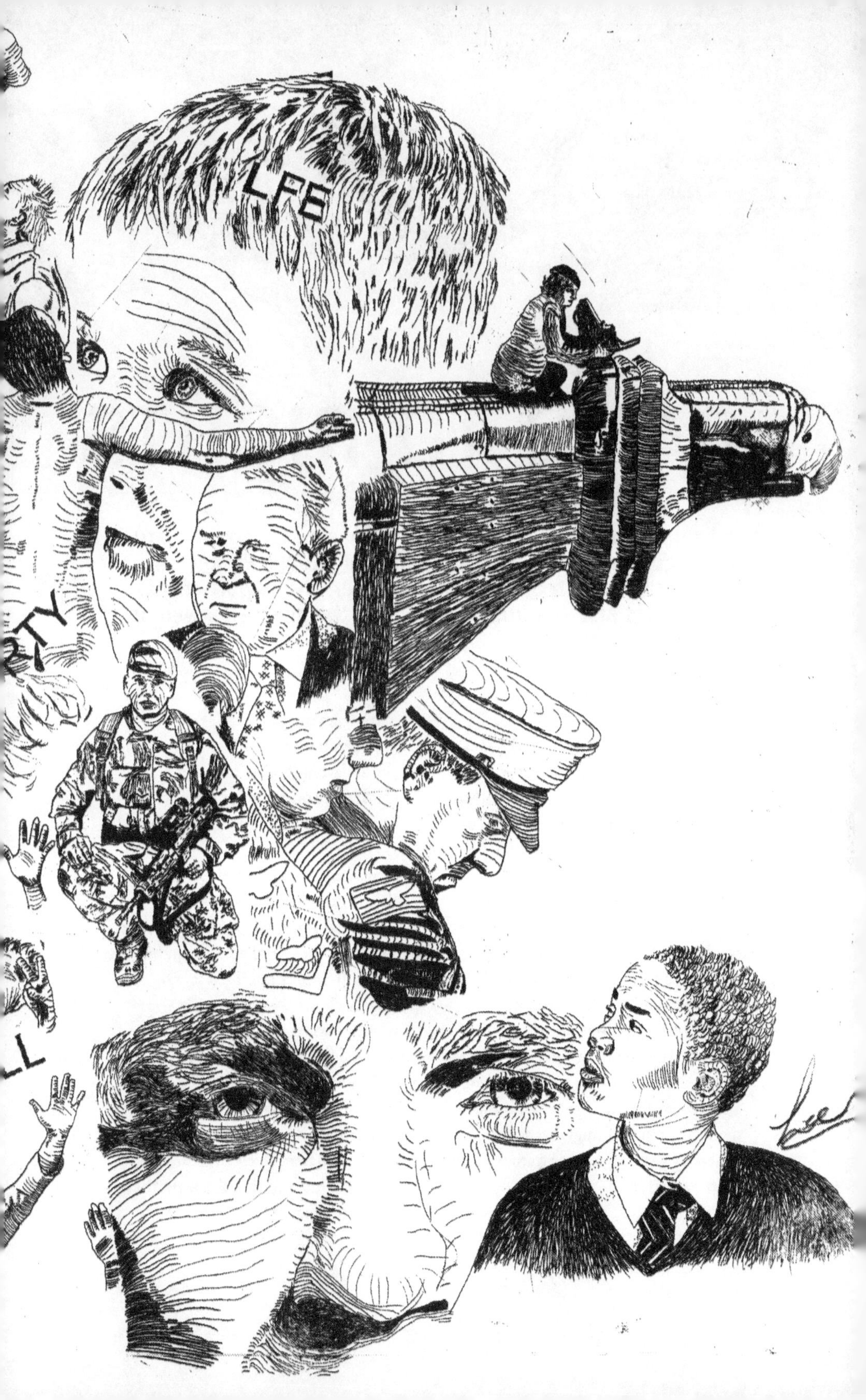
LFE
RTY
LL

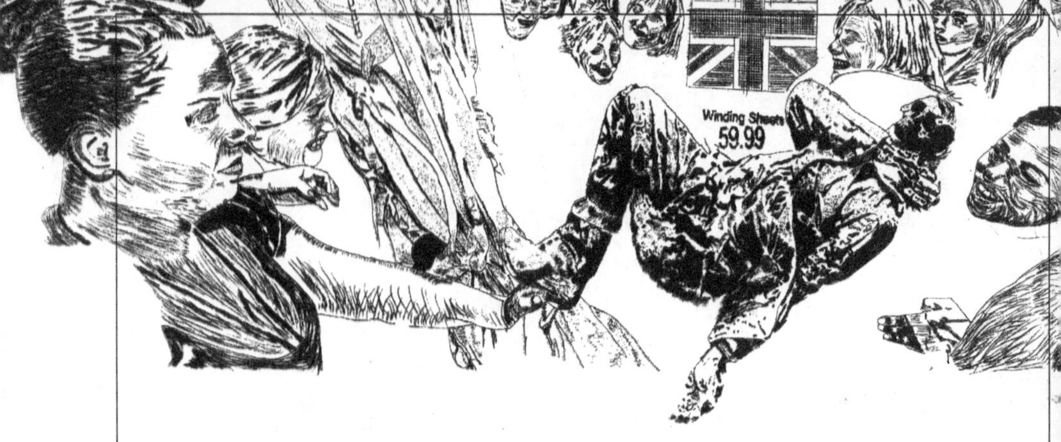

BANG TO RIGHTS

In light of Strangers into Citizens' campaign for an amnesty for 'illegals' in the UK, <u>Camille Barbagallo</u> & <u>Nic Beuret</u> consider how such an act of 'generosity' on the part of the state would also reaffirm its power as the giver – as well as denier – of rights

O n 7 May 2007 several thousand 'migrants' (some with papers, some without) mobilised and took part in an ongoing campaign, coordinated in the main by religious groups and community organisations, for an amnesty for 'illegals' currently living in the UK. While rough surveys amongst the crowd showed that most people were there to support the idea of an amnesty – an amnesty without limitations – that was not the point of the rally, nor the mass held beforehand. In fact the rally was organised as part of a campaign for managed migration, made on behalf of migrants without papers by a group called Strangers into Citizens (SiC):

Strangers into Citizens is a campaign by the Citizen Organising Foundation (COF), an alliance of faith and community organizations across London and in Birmingham.[1]

To explore the question of 'organising' with and amongst people without papers, we wish to use as our departure point those 'illegals' the SiC amnesty supposedly speaks for. That is, not those people who work illegally, without national insurance numbers, those who avoid paying tax, or work in illegal industries, but those who are in the UK without visas or papers that would give them the legal right to remain. In making such a distinction, we are not claiming that the work they do or their 'illegality' is essentially

One grants rights – just like one welcomes strangers. It's a gift that can't be reciprocated

different to other people who labour and/or live illegally; rather we believe that there exists a continuum along which labour and life enter into a problematic with legality (or 'become illegal'). And though it would be interesting to see how much of life and labour in the UK is always already 'becoming illegal' (and concretely how people seek to 'go illegal' as a survival strategy), we will stay with those 'strangers' that SiC want to help become citizens. Both because of the specifics of the SiC campaign and because of the problematic posed by migrants without papers. We also need to be clear that there is no singular migrant subjectivity or category: the migrant is defined at best as a particular kind of 'temporary' subjectivity or social relation – temporary, even if it lasts for a lifetime, because of its transitory nature. Positing and organising migrants as though they were

homogeneous or in possession of a singular subjectivity with specifically 'migrant' characteristics is in many ways the first step to policing and controlling them.

We believe that those who have been here for four or more years should be admitted to a two-year pathway to full legal rights ('leave to remain') during which they work legally and demonstrate their contribution to UK economy and society.

Regularization will help to expose these undesirables, enabling authorities to concentrate resources on removing them – and not the honest, hard-working people who are making Britain great.[2]

What is important here is not the glaring contradiction between a faith based group effectively asking of their object of charity 'what's in it for us' (as if charity was ever anything other than self-serving) or the vile nationalism of church-led nation building. It is important rather to focus on the struggle such a discourse obscures. On the one hand state and capital attempt to organise a body of people to both profit from them and to reproduce capital and the nation through them. On the other hand, that same body of people struggle for access to institutions, social wealth and the potential to live 'free' from certain

---

　　　　All images by Lee Galpin　　　　

kinds of arbitrary violence (whether it be the violence of the state or capital). Here we need to focus on the discourse of rights and citizenship, their interrelation and limits, and how, in reality, the SiC's proposal for amnesty is not so far from the UN 'ideal' of a fully implemented and binding international charter on human rights.

Amnesties, Citizens & the People

The conception of human rights based upon the assumed existence of a human being as such, broke down at the very moment when those who professed to believe in it were for the first time confronted with people who had indeed lost all other qualities and specific relationships – except that they were still human. The world found nothing sacred in the abstract nakedness of the human being.[3]

One grants rights – just like one welcomes strangers. It's a gift that can't be reciprocated – a gesture of power, of ownership and an assertion of the primary right. I have the right to give you rights, to grant you asylum, to welcome you into 'my' territory and all on my terms. It is a gift that one must be grateful for, but not one that was necessarily asked for. That one has to have arrived first is a matter of course

for the most part (though not always). One arrives, and then applies for a visa, asylum, etc. The process of welcoming or granting reverses this moment, re-inscribes the primacy of the state and/or 'native' citizen with relation to the stranger without papers or rights, erasing the fact that the 'stranger' arrived without asking permission, and stayed without leave. Which, of course, is exactly the problem: the arrival and claim without prior permission or 'right' threatens the entire system, puts it into jeopardy. They are an 'invading horde' until they have been realised as victims or 'good-intentioned hard-working people' not too dissimilar from us (though not the same of course, so we have to be 'tolerant'). An amnesty then, is an attempt to neutralise a threat – the threat of those without a specific status who usurp the primacy of the state and its native population.

The assertion of primacy posits a body of people that exist with certain rights with regards to each other and the territory they inhabit: the citizenry and their rights. The SiC amnesty not only manages migrant bodies insofar as it orders them as bodies and manages their unruly moment of uninvited and unmanaged movement – it also reproduces the citizen and the native. It reproduces 'the people'. We the 'British', as good fair people who have a tradition of generosity and fairness, who are not only capable of granting these poor people amnesty but welcoming them into our society, as

The other is made in the same moment as 'the native', producing both tolerance and racism (as if they were really that distinct)

long as they subscribe to our values. This is the discourse produced by the SiC amnesty. A racist discourse (in the sense of producing a race of people with values, histories, and certain 'powers', not to mention the assumed white skin colour…). The amnesty produces 'the people' as much as it homogenises the migrant – it sets up a twin moment of re/production, hinging on a notion of tolerance. Little wonder then that its corollary is a crude racism. The other is made in the same moment as 'the native', producing both tolerance and racism (as if they were really that distinct).

Of course, the racism produced by such moments also has a directly productive role with regards to capital. Race is one of the key differentials in the wage and labour hierarchy. Amnesties generally serve as momentary corrections to national labour markets, serving the needs of capital in a crude, safety valve kind of way. Of course it is not that illegality does not also serve the needs of capital, but it does so in a different fashion. In the economic instance, an amnesty serves to bring into the formal economy (for reasons of taxation and management) those people working outside of it. To be sure there are markets and economies that benefit significantly from illegality, but nonetheless this illegality needs to be constantly managed and when it is not necessary, the illegal must be brought into the legal. This movement back and forth, between legal and illegal is by no means a smooth space and while illegality benefits the interests of certain sections of capital, it is also worth noting it is not always the view of the state managers of the national economy that illegality is of benefit.

But amnesties are not just economic corrections. Amnesties rarely come without conditions – the SiC proposal is not unusual in that it requires that to receive papers under the amnesty one needs to fulfil certain conditions – the conditions of a limited citizenship based on the performance of the willing and worthy applicant: hard working, family orientated, etc., exactly the sort of person that could and should be accepted into the social body. It not only reproduces the people through the moment of racialised antagonism, but produces them anew from the migrant population.

Rights & Social Wealth

It's no longer novel or indeed that useful to argue the obvious fact that rights and rights discourse are not something that humans as a species 'have', or could be said to have: they are in fact citizen's rights, insofar as they are conventions, ethical and moral dictates, laws and legislations by a particular state for its citizens. That there has been a degree of harmonisation via such supra-governmental bodies as the UN and through the construction of an international human rights discourse enacted by humanitarian missions and NGOs, does not fundamentally detract from the point that bereft of a state and of citizenship, human rights lack an agent to assure them. Without the state's violence, it does not make sense to speak of rights that are protected or assured.

Rights are fundamentally modes of being in relation to the nation state (and the international system of nation-states, as well as the canon of western liberal thought and the transnational

bereft of a state and of citizenship, human rights lack an agent to assure them

organisation of governance), protected to varying degrees by that same state. One could say (following Foucault) that human rights are a milieu created by the never-resolved relation between a state and the bodies it governs in order to manage the circulation of struggles, relations and properties within it (security and rights being both part of a biopolitical regime). That they have been internationalised does not mean they are any less localised in a particular state. And as Giorgio Agamben has shown, it is through such a production that life is inscribed in the nation-state (both judicially and through the production of a 'people' with 'rights' – and presumably 'obligations').

However, this is not to say that rights do not exist, or that they are not without use: rights are largely the result of struggle and a counter-violence against the state. The fact that they represent the re-inscription of life in the nation-state, and the management

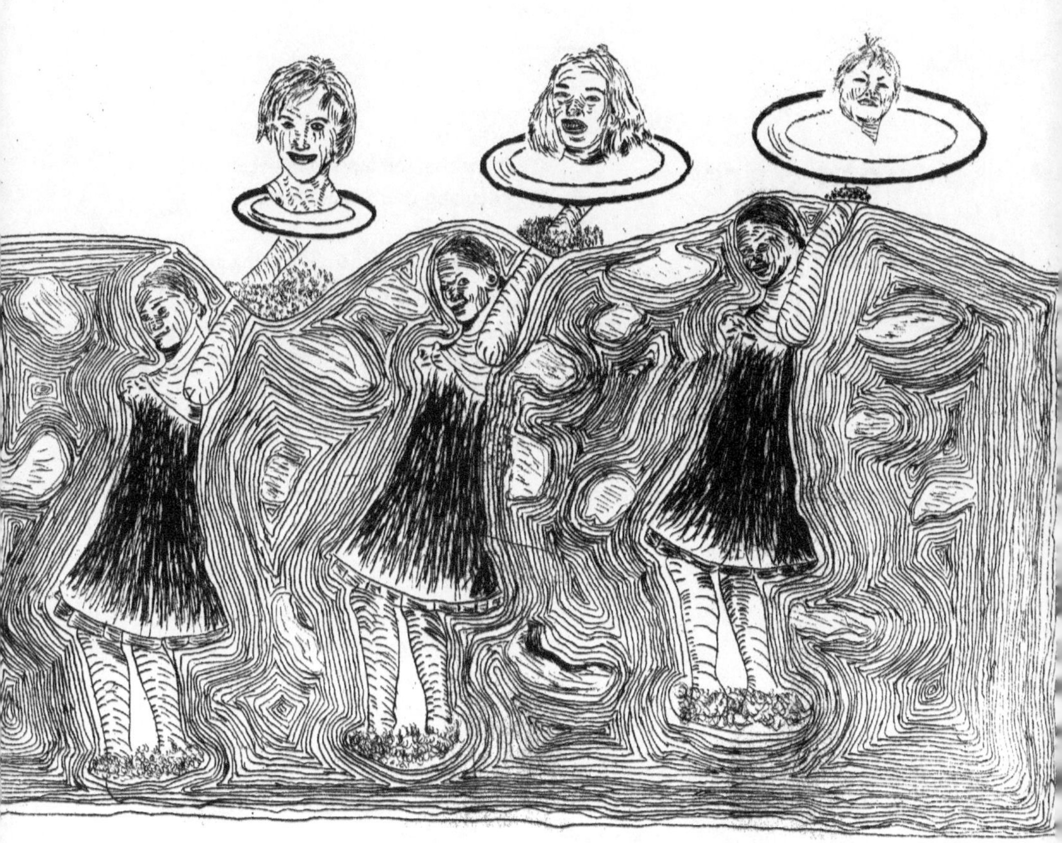

of labour and life for capital, does not mean they do not also represent real gains and victories. It is never all or nothing. There is nothing predetermined or linear about the process of decoding/recoding, de-institutionalisation/re-institutionalisation. And more importantly. while rights are a discourse of citizens and states, this does not mean that therefore rights and the discourse of rights are useless or meaningless for those who find themselves without papers or stateless. The citizen and the state are not smooth spaces: the citizen is always partial and contested, quite often by those bodies that are not even considered human, let alone members of a political community.

In the final instance, both the citizen and the state require outsides – the citizen requires the non-citizen, and the state requires the border to define it and its limits (we could also say the nation requires both the people and those that exist contrary to the spirit of the people…). The figure of the refugee, the migrant and the foreign criminal play important roles in the maintenance and re/construction of them all. There is a necessary outside.

rights are largely the result of struggle and a counter-violence against the state

But this necessary outside must be constantly in the process of breaching the boundaries and coming inside. The maintenance of the figures and spaces of the state, nation, citizen and people are not guaranteed merely by the existence of an outside but by the constant threat of contamination and exchange. The boundaries and borders must be crossed and threatened for the categories to have meaning. This shows the deeper state-building significance of an amnesty – it is a state-led and managed moment of controlling and organising the tension and threat in a productive way for both the state and capital. An amnesty might represent a real and substantial gain for migrant communities and a limited number of individuals, but at the cost of the re-inscription of life into the state and the legitimisation of the state's role in managing the tension between, and circulation across, borders and boundaries.

The aim of the SiC campaign was for an amnesty that resulted in managed migration: however, the aim of the campaign for the participating migrants was not necessarily citizenship, but rather to gain papers that would create some certainties, access to social wealth and legal working conditions within the UK. Papers do not necessarily mean citizenship: quite often people don't want citizenship, but prefer to keep a pre-existing one. Citizenship – on paper or in the sense of a relation to the state – is always incomplete however. Part of the management of the circulation of bodies within the space of citizenship – from one end of the axis to the other – is organising the space of rights and obligations of citizens. For the state, rights and obligations are not merely means to organise the behaviour and economic performances of its population, but a means to create a particular kind of people through the production of a national milieu or discourse over what citizens do and don't do, what kinds of people belong to the state, and ultimately what this state 'is' and means with regards to forms of life. But from the point of view of the migrant, rights codify a certain kind of access to social wealth – institutional and waged. From medical care to minimum wages, they codify access (or the potential for access).

Pushing Up Against the Limits

There are obvious limits to the amnesty – more often than not it merely serves the processes of managed migration and does little to ensure stability or security for migrants. Moreover, it recreates the nation and the people and re-institutionalises the very moments of the stratification of citizenship (via race, gender, language, education, class, etc.). It is also obvious that the amnesty does little for those migrants who have no wish to be 'visible' for whatever reason (working in stigmatised industries, working in illegal or untaxed industries, being undesirable from the point of view of the state and capital, etc.). It needs to be noted that quite often the push for an amnesty comes after a cycle of struggles, strikes, riots and refusals and so serves as a channel towards legitimate institutional processes and procedures and away from potentially more radical and threatening modes of resistance (though it should be added that there is nothing inherently radical or progressive about riots or non-institutional political events – obviously their character depends on the forms of social organisation from which they emerge).

But the amnesty too can also produce a new set of subjects able to access social wealth and engage in the process of destabilising and contesting the existing 'social contract' and class relations from a stronger position of power. The re-inscription of life into the law and the reproduction of the state and capital are not without threats of their own. Perhaps one of the most powerful examples of the threatening aspect of the pursuit of rights was the slave revolts of Haiti that brought the Napoleonic regime to its knees and shook the foundations of Europe, all under the guise of the slaves' pursuit of the 'rights of man'.

Footnotes

1 http://www.strangersintocitizens.org.uk

2 Ibid.

3 Hannah Arendt, 'The Decline of the Nation-State and the End of the Rights of Man', in *The Origins of Totalitarianism*, New York: Harvest, 1976, 267-302.

Nicholas <diasporas@gmail.com> and Camille <elli.maci@gmail.com> have recently migrated to Europe, live in East London and have worked on migration and labour issues in Australia and the UK. They continue to be interested in migration as a social movement, its intersection with gender and the imposition of neocolonial technologies in the metropole

ORGANISING IN THE DARK:

INTERVIEWS ABOUT MIGRANTS' STRUGGLES

Workers' struggles to improve conditions traditionally voice demands for visibility, rights and citizenship. But when visibility brings with it the risk of detention and deportation other strategies may be necessary. Equally, when rights are dependent on the whims of employers, how desirable are they? The experience of migration and illegality is multiple and contingent on the resources of class, race, gender and income. Campaigns and struggles therefore cohere around diverse experiences, involve different levels of risk and confrontation, and mobilise such disparate groups as church congregations, community groups, activist networks, unions, mosques, and national associations. The tactics and positions employed entail conflicting ideas about whether or not to collaborate with the state. Here Jaya Klara Brekke talks to four UK based groups working to improve conditions for migrants and asks 'how does one organise in the dark?' Their answers describe the day to day experience of a tightening immigration system and responses to it, from direct resistance and support work to proposals for reform

　　　　All images by Harrisson　　　　

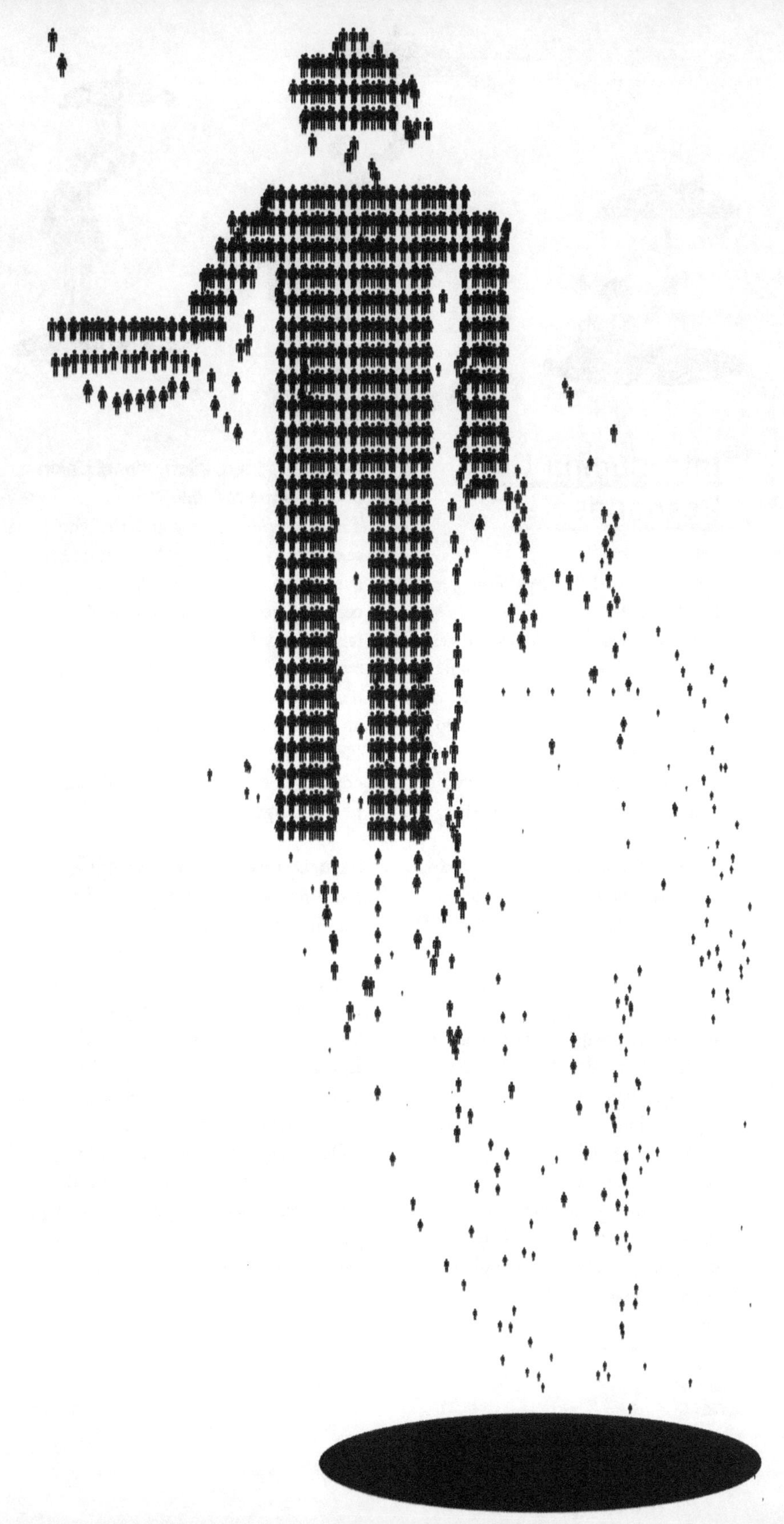

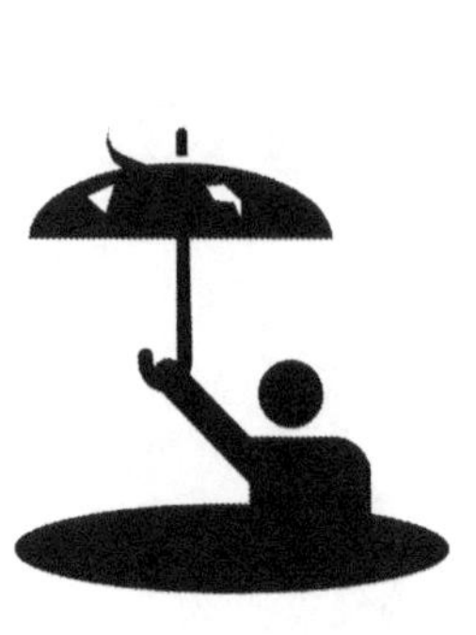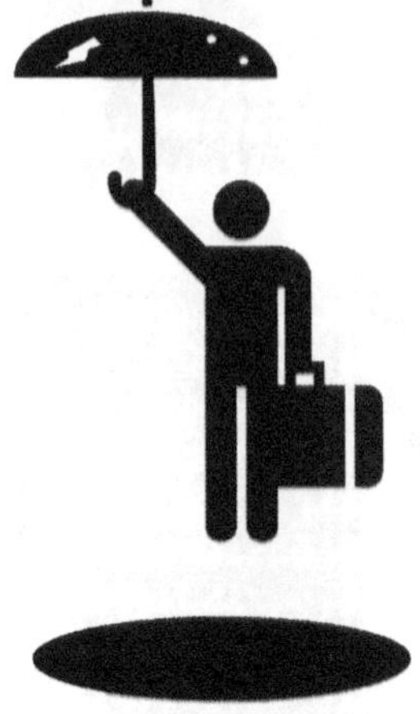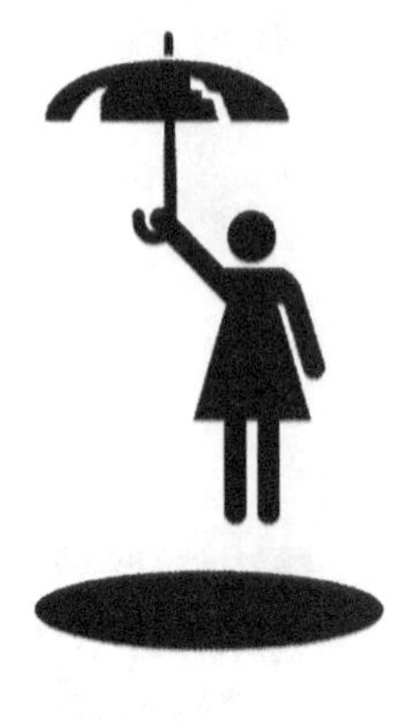

Introducing the Respondents:

Sean Bamford, Trade Union Congress (TUC):

Sean Bamford is the Policy Officer of Migration. The TUC holds conferences on migration and publish reports on the conditions of migrant workers and the effects of government policies, as well as working for migrants and advising them about their rights at work.

Matthew Bolton, Strangers into Citizens and The East London Communities Organisation (TELCO):

TELCO is a campaign platform for community groups, putting pressure on politicians, providing training in building campaigns and community leadership. It consists of churches, mosques, schools and other community organisations. TELCO started the Strangers into Citizens campaign, which proposes a pathway for the regularisation of undocumented migrant workers in the UK with a focus on rights, legality, and changing the negative image of migrant workers in the media.

Ava Caradonna, International Union of Sex Workers (IUSW)

The IUSW organises across the whole sex industry, traversing illegal and legal occupations. It operates within a complex area where conditions of legality and illegality, race and class overlap and are intensified. The 'double illegality' of someone working both in an illegal industry as well has having an illegal immigration status poses a challenge on all fronts to traditional political organising.

Sara, London No Borders (NB):

No Borders is an anti-capitalist direct action network organising campaigns and actions against borders and border controls. They provide 'on the ground' detainee support, activist support in union campaigns for migrant workers' rights, and monitoring in reporting centres. No Borders carry out actions against detention centres, and collaborate with other organisations and activist groups around the needs and conditions of migrants and people in asylum. They produce a transnational newsletter entitled *Papers For All*.

The Terms of Visibility

Jaya Brekke: Conventionally, union struggle is built on rights, visibility and being out on the streets, but how does one organise in an illegal industry among people who may also have an illegal immigration status, where visibility could mean imprisonment and deportation?

Ava Caradonna, International Union of Sex Workers (IUWS): The name 'Ava Caradonna' is a collective name used by activists in the International Sex Workers Union to find productive ways to engage with the stigma of being associated with selling sex. In terms of visibility it is about playing with what it means to be invisible, and finding ways of being visible that aren't necessarily about the individual. I think this is one way to cut across illegality, and it means that both legal and illegal people can organise in the same place. It is not easy to organise in the sex industry. This is something that needs to be recognised from the outset. Combating the social isolation and stigma that sex workers feel is a big part of what 'workplace' organising is. When you are organising with people who are so marginalised and so hidden, you can't conceptualise around workplace organising within traditional models of, for example, putting pressure on employers, because it will result in violence in a really

'it's about finding ways of being visible that aren't about the individual'

horrible way. There are certainly a lot of sex workers, but the ability to draw them together into some kind of coherent subjectivity is pretty hard. Many people don't really assume the identity of 'sex worker', but that is not to say that sex workers themselves don't have networks, that they don't organise, and they don't move in certain ways that are outside leftist politics and trade union struggles. People have a whole variety of strategies to deal with issues and conditions around safety within the industry such as moving to employers that are better and passing on information. At a day-to-day level the networks are made and practical projects are being identified around significant needs, and these are things we can do without having to draw people into visibility. I don't think that visibility, legality and citizenship are necessarily only one moment.

JB: How did the Strangers into Citizens campaign come about?

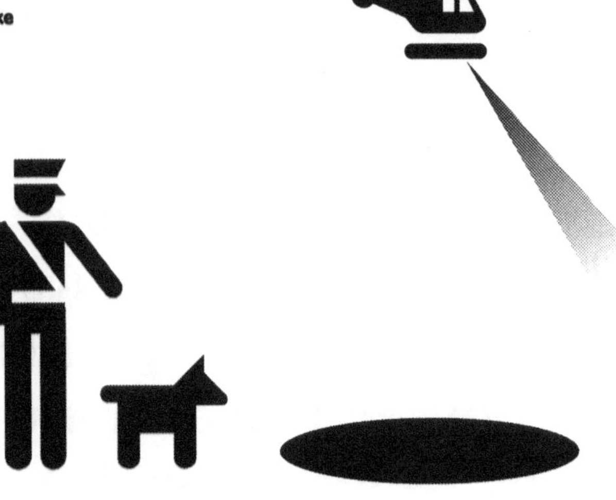

Matthew Bolton, Strangers into Citizens (SiC): The Strangers into Citizens campaign sprung out of our other campaigns for housing and the living wage. We realised more and more that people in our churches, schools and communities were affected by immigration policies. It took a long time and many discussions among our members to agree to set up Strangers into Citizens, as many people saw it as being way too radical. But after many public talks where migrants spoke out about their conditions as living with illegal status or under the threat of deportation, and people saw that they actually are friends, neighbours or colleagues, we were able to develop and start this campaign. But it was difficult because we are an extremely diverse organisation where you have some people that might be church based, who one would consider conservative or Tory in their politics, but have a very liberal take on some social issues. And then you might have a Mosque heavily critical of market-based economics but which might be quite conservative

when it comes to social issues. Often media or politicians will call up and ask about our position on some issue, but TELCO does not have a position on things, we work only on specific causes. Our members are so diverse that if we were to take positions on things we would end up spending all our time discussing and fighting about them, and have no time for actually doing anything!

JB: What are the long term goals of a one-off campaign like Strangers into Citizens?

Matthew Bolton (SiC): The long term goals are firstly to build up our membership and capacity. Through this campaign we will hopefully get stronger and bigger as an organisation, which is the most important thing because if we are not strong as an organisation we cannot achieve anything.

JB: What are some of the specific changes or developments that trade

'if unions don't embrace diversity we will be a declining force'

unions have undergone when having to consider organising migrants, especially undocumented ones?

Sean Bamford, Trade Union Congress (TUC): We are a country that is used to migration, although the present wave of migration is different because migrants are coming from different parts of the world than before. For the union movement there is an element of self-interest in that if we don't embrace diversity we will be an increasingly declining force within the workplace. That is the pragmatic side of it. The ethical side is that we see our mission as achieving fairness within the workplace. So our concern about migrants and the most recent wave of migrants is located within that wider perspective.

JB: What are the main activities and long term goals of No Borders (NB)?

Sara, No Borders (NB): Our politics and where we are coming from is a desire to have freedom of movement for all, to have no border controls, and to ultimately have no capitalism and no nation states. However, in order to achieve something here and now and in the world we live in, we don't have a campaign against capitalism or states, but have medium term and short term goals, such as anti-deportation work and closing down detention centres, and we use different strategies aimed at realising those goals. Even if we don't stop the new detention centre near Gatwick airport from being built, through the campaign we are learning, building up a network, trying to develop different tactics, building links with the migrants that are directly affected, researching into the companies that are involved in the detention industries and starting a process of developing action against those companies.

Rights or Wrongs?

JB: What does legality and illegality mean on an everyday level? Class, language, race and so on play a big role. How useful is it to organise around these terms?

Ava Caradonna (IUSW): In a completely deregulated sector there are no rules around how things are actually run. The only way that rules are abided by is either through threats or violence or coercion of some kind, which you could also say about many other 'normal' jobs. The debate about trafficking and by default prostitution is dominated and contextualised by legislation, research and a moral position that selling and purchasing sex is something that is fundamentally wrong. That it is damaging to the 'women' involved and to society more generally. And I think it is very much about legality and illegality, and about policing women's migration. Two weeks ago the UK Human Trafficking Centre launched Operation Pentameter 2, the UK government/law enforcement response to human trafficking which focuses on prostitution. It involves the raiding, arrest and 'rescuing' of migrant sex workers who are classified as trafficked victims. So there are raids and deportations going on. I think that such police operations can be understood clearly as controlling and 'policing' the boundaries of legality and illegality. At the centre of concepts of 'victims and criminals' is the need to 'protect' migrant women and 'punish' migrant men. Casting good migrants against bad ('illegals'), really only creates the conditions that ensure and maintain exploitation in the sex industry and ensures that there will always be this stream of exploitative migrant labour to the UK.

JB: Are there ways of enforcing your rights when you are illegal?

Sean Bamford (TUC): I think I can say that in the UK at the moment there are

'where migrants take action for themselves the 'victim'/'resource' stereotype is challenged'

not. And this is a massive problem because some employers don't exactly fall into employing undocumented workers by accident. There is some evidence that the particularly unscrupulous go for them because they know they can exploit them; they know they have got no recourse to the courts etc. We would ideally like to move towards a separation in the legal system between actual rights of workers and the person's status of residency and work permit. But at the moment there is a problem for the employee – 'will I end up being deported if I go to court?' The enforcement of rights is a big issue, because the trade union movement is patchy in terms of identity, and we have an imbalance where we are stronger in the public than the private sector. This is not a problem for the more skilled migrants going into areas of public sector administration, the NHS, and indeed for those highly skilled workers going into IT, partly because they have real economic clout. I think the problem lies where you have a lack of union organisation together with the fact that many of these workers are easily replaceable, in the sense that if you are pulling up carrots from a field and there are other people available to do it, you are not in a terribly strong position. Government is sitting down with us to look at the issue of enforcement. If the laws are there we must have the means by which to enforce them.

JB: When viewed in a 'positive' light by media and state, migrants are portrayed and treated either as an economic resource, or as victims. Are there ways people are taking action that do not rely on these two stereotypes?

Sara (NB): Yes, where either economic migrants or asylum seekers stand up and take action for themselves and demand things. This challenges those stereotypes. And particularly when people in detention take action. For example, when quite a few people recently escaped from Campsfield [Campsfield House, a notorious 'immigration removal centre' in Oxfordshire opened in 1993], and also the large scale riot in November in Harmondsworth detention centre,

where they destroyed a 200 capacity building in the detention complex. There have been several reports recently about how undocumented workers are contributing to the economy, while there is huge scaremongering by the government and the mainstream media against asylum seekers and how they are a drain on resources to the point where people really hate them. With the points-based system and the possibility of an amnesty for economic migrants, I do think they are moving towards a professionalisation of migration, selecting who is useful, who has the particular skill-sets necessary, etc. In the case of asylum seekers there are many legal challenges that you can mount when you are facing deportation. But if someone is an undocumented worker it is a lot more difficult because there are almost no legal options. No Borders doesn't make any political distinction between political and economic migrants, we support undocumented workers as much as asylum seekers but on a practical level it is much more difficult because they are not out in the open and don't have the same networks of assistance.

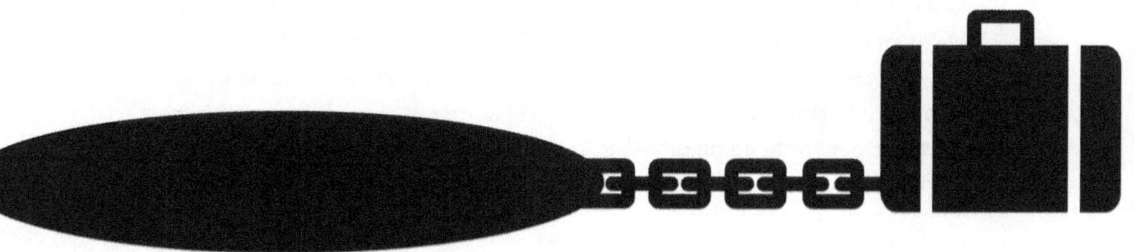

JB: Could you briefly describe your proposal for an amnesty for illegal workers?

Matthew Bolton (SiC): We are asking that those who have been here for four or more years are admitted to a two-year pathway to full legal rights ('leave to remain'). During that period they will work legally, whereby they can demonstrate their contribution to UK economy and society.

JB: What is the reason for the four-year criteria?

MB: The four-year period, with the fifth trial year is set because we see it as a realistic target. It is based on the fact that people who come to the country legally to work can extend their permit to stay up to five years, and then apply for leave to remain. And so we can't really ask for fewer than the five years for people who enter illegally because then one would argue that we are rewarding the illegals. So what we are campaigning for is that whether you have entered the country illegally, are an over-stayer or have become illegal after having your asylum case refused, if you have been here for five years you can enter this pathway, go through the two year trial period and then apply for leave to remain. After the two trial years you need to show that you have not committed any serious crime (and here it is important to emphasise that any crime related to papers will not

count as a serious crime!) and you have a sponsor. This could be an employer, but not necessarily, because that would place too much power in the hands of the employer, so also a colleague, a priest or someone in your community – someone who can vouch for you.

JB: Do you support Strangers into Citizens proposal for 'regularisation' of immigrants (legal residency and identity documents) and amnesty?

Sara (NB): In the London No Borders group we had a lot of discussion about this and were very divided on the issue. It is a hard thing because it is not just a demand coming from Strangers into Citizens; it is also coming from a lot of migrants themselves. When you are working with people that are facing deportation or detention on a day-to-day level, anything that will help some of them is something you would support. However, the conditions that are attached to the proposal are problematic. You will have a lot of people coming out in the hope that they will get amnesty, but many will be refused and then be facing deportation. What we might see is that people who are most directly in the firing line, often families who are failed asylum

'we are asking for a two-year pathway to full legal rights'

seekers because they can't go underground, are to be the first people who get rounded up and deported. Also, amnesties are generally coupled with a stronger clamp down. David Blunkett in 1997 proposed an amnesty for some people, coupled with ID cards and much stronger border controls for everyone else, and with a total crack down on migrants afterwards.

But one thing that was very positive about the Strangers into Citizens campaign was the 7th May march, which to my knowledge was the first public march of undocumented workers that there has been in London. It brought people out of the shadows, out on the streets together and gave people confidence. So whatever we thought about their proposal, we went to the march and it was a great opportunity to engage with these people.

Finally, I think it is a problem when you have a campaign asking for so little. The position we eventually came to in No Borders was to ask for papers for all and to not leave anyone out. Because we see it as our job to make the demands, and not enter a situation where we are the ones proposing the parameters that in the end are established by governments. Imagine somebody who can prove they have been here for four years, who can prove that they have been working, whose employer is willing to stand up and say 'yes, this person has been working for

me illegally', who can speak English, when English for Speakers of Other Languages (ESOL) classes are being cut back: it is going to be hardly anyone. So, yes, an amnesty will help some people, but personally I would not get into the business of excluding and setting the governments parameters for it.

JB: Do you support proposals for amnesty such as those of Strangers into Citizens and the Joint Council of Welfare of Immigrants?

Sean Bamford (TUC): The TUC doesn't have a position on amnesty. I think it is an interesting discussion and certainly we want to be part of it. No one knows the exact amount of undocumented workers but the estimate is 600,000 people. There is no way that the government has the resources to get rid of 600 thousand people from this country, and given that they are going to have some

'sex work does provide a way of making fuckloads more money than domestic work'

dependants etc. we could be talking about a million. It would also be deeply unsavoury to say the least, if not incredibly distressing! This is where there are double standards: on the one hand we deny these people a right including their rights to be here, and on the other hand there are sections of the economy that depend very heavily on such workers to do the jobs they are doing.

JB: Do you know of the Strangers into Citizens campaign for amnesty?

Ava Caradonna (IUSW): Yes. I don't think anyone is really including the sex workers in their amnesty proposal. That is a classic example of who is excluded from such proposals.

JB: Is it possible to work towards larger structural changes and long term goals with illegalised people and work places?

AC: In terms of larger structural changes, sex workers are a long way behind a lot of people in things like having decent working conditions, stability, a pension, and real things that make a difference in how people can make decisions in their lives. But I

think that sex work to a large degree and for lots and lots of migrant women does provide a way of making fuckloads more money than if you were a domestic worker or a cleaner. We are talking about £100 per hour easily, maybe £50 per hour, substantially more than £3.50! So it does actually translate into good things for people – being able to send a good amount of money home or be able to pay for dreams and projects of their own. This situation only exists because the industry is so illegalised and stigmatised; in fact some process of visibility in the sex industry would be somewhat threatening to this – for example, if it was legalised the state would tax it. In that kind of way it's not that the state manages work well, prostitution remains an incredibly coercive environment to work in. The Netherlands are a perfect example, and so is Australia – their legal brothels are just as exploitative as working in London, but of course there you don't run the same risk of being arrested. What we are really talking about is criminalisation. In somewhere like London where the industry is so diversified, even something like prostitution is so racialised that where you end up in the hierarchy has a lot to do with whether or not you have papers.

JB: The immigration system is changing a lot with increasing incarceration and the introduction of the points-based system. How does that affect the way you work with migrants?

Sean Bamford (TUC): We accept that there is a need to have a system in place that manages migration from outside the EU. However, we want to ensure that such a system is fair and respects workers and indeed human rights. And we have had problems both with the existent system and the one that is going to replace it. To give two examples: the work permit system effectively ties an individual employee to an individual employer. This is a contravention of workers rights, where the employer invariably has more control over the situation than the worker. If the employee feels he is being abused he cannot just walk away and sell his labour elsewhere, because he could get kicked out of the country for breaching the terms of his work permit. This gives too much power to the employer. Also, in tier three of the points based system, which regulates the less skilled workers that they want to bring into certain sectors like agriculture, people have no right to bring relatives into the UK. That is in contravention of the right to family life. And I could go on and on. We are hoping for equality in the way people are selected, so that the system once it

is in place will be free of bias. I think it is about joining together and saying that there are a lot of us out there that are concerned about migrant workers, how can we work together to actually support these people? In our case, get them into the union because that is the clearest way that they will have protection in the workplace.

Beyond Pragmatism

JB: In what way does everyday organising translate into long term transformations? For example, could you explain your project, x:talk?

Ava Caradonna (IUSW): X:talk [pronounced- cross talk] involves teaching English based around language needed in the sex industry to migrant sex-workers. It is run from an NHS sexual health clinic in central London, once a week over the course of three months covering topics such as health, dealing with employers and customers, what they do and don't do, how much they charge and so on. It is specifically for sex workers, you don't have to say what kind of immigration status you have, and it is free. It is in recognition of the fact that 60-70 percent of the sex workers in London are migrants, so it is not some minority we are talking about. We did x:talk because it was the type of project we could do that was practical, that would

enable us to make networks and contact with migrant communities. I was sick of having ideological conversations and tried to think of what were some of the root causes of sexual exploitation and meaningful ways in which those things could change the power dynamics. But I don't think that x:talk is really entering a debate around, or directly challenging, legality and illegality. It does run the risk of becoming simply a service that can be co-opted really easily in the running and maintenance of the current border regime. Yet we have decided that language is really central to organising, so it is a building block to greater ideas and possibilities.

JB: You have recently become part of GMB Trade Union. What are the benefits and limitations of this?

AC: The IUSW became part of the GMB in 2000 so it has actually been quite a while now. And in many ways the branch has left us completely alone. There was the first unfair dismissal case in the sex-industry for firing a sex-worker recently. But that kind of stuff is just weird, it is not the reality of how the GMB works. I think of it more as a very important thing to have on paper. And I use it as such.

JB: Is the organising of sex workers limited to a very pragmatic level, or is there space to go beyond that? Do you have political goals on a broader level?

AC: Not here at the moment, no. But is there any movement that is ready for that now here in the Global North? I think people are ready to make alliances.

JB: Can everyday pragmatic organising and campaigns translate into, or provide a basis for, long term transformations?

Sara (NB): This has been a big discussion in the London No Borders group. When focusing on anti-deportation and detainee support on an individual level it was very hard to look at and fight the asylum system as a whole. Nevertheless, this work enables us to make contact with people inside the detention centres. So when there was a hunger strike of Zimbabwean women in detention that went across multiple detention centres, those who were doing detainee support could visit the different detention centres, give them phone cards and put them in touch with each other. All those people were released. And this was not on an individual level, but a struggle that we were able to support won by the Zimbabwean women collectively. When we started to do regular demonstrations outside Colnbrook and Harmondsworth detention centres, we were able to distribute leaflets inside the centres because of our previous visits there. During the demonstrations people were ringing us from inside and telling us 'the guards are locking us in our rooms', 'the guards are beating us and not letting us come to the windows'.

Another example of work that has been really successful is No Borders in Glasgow as part of the Unity coalition. The Unity coalition set up an office opposite the reporting centre in Glasgow, and everyone who went into the reporting centre first of all could leave their children there, because they can't detain you if you don't have your children with you. Also everyone who went inside would first write their name down at the Unity office and then cross their name off after, so that they could ring around to contacts and start support work immediately if a name was not crossed off by the end of the day. It was a relatively new thing in Glasgow to have asylum seekers, so once people living alongside them found out what they had been through there was a huge amount of community support. People were doing lookouts and letting them hide in their houses. They managed to make dawn raids in houses of failed asylum seekers completely unworkable to the point where they stopped altogether. Successful campaigns that help people on a small everyday level empower many of the asylum seekers themselves to support each other and organise and get involved, as well as local people.

And in the case of Glasgow, it had the actual effect of making a government policy unworkable. So I think that at the moment we need to work in a more structurally focused way and create networks that are powerful enough to have a lasting effect.

Info

International Union of Sex Workers:
http://www.iusw.org/

No Borders Network:
http://www.noborder.org/

Strangers into Citizens:
http://www.strangersintocitizens.org.uk

TUC:
http://www.tuc.org.uk/

Jaya Klara Brekke <jayapapaya@gmail.com>, together with Dagmar Diesner, recently released Underground Londoners, a documentary addressing the life, working conditions and struggles of undocumented migrants working as cleaners in the London Underground. She waitresses, teaches, does graphic work for the journal Occupied London and works on other media and performance projects in London and Copenhagen

PUTTING ILLEGALITY TO WORK

The vulnerability of illegalised workers forces them to accept the worst pay and conditions and produces conflict within the working class as a whole. Here <u>Seemab Gul</u> examines how the production of this illegality is the main goal of the UK's immigration laws

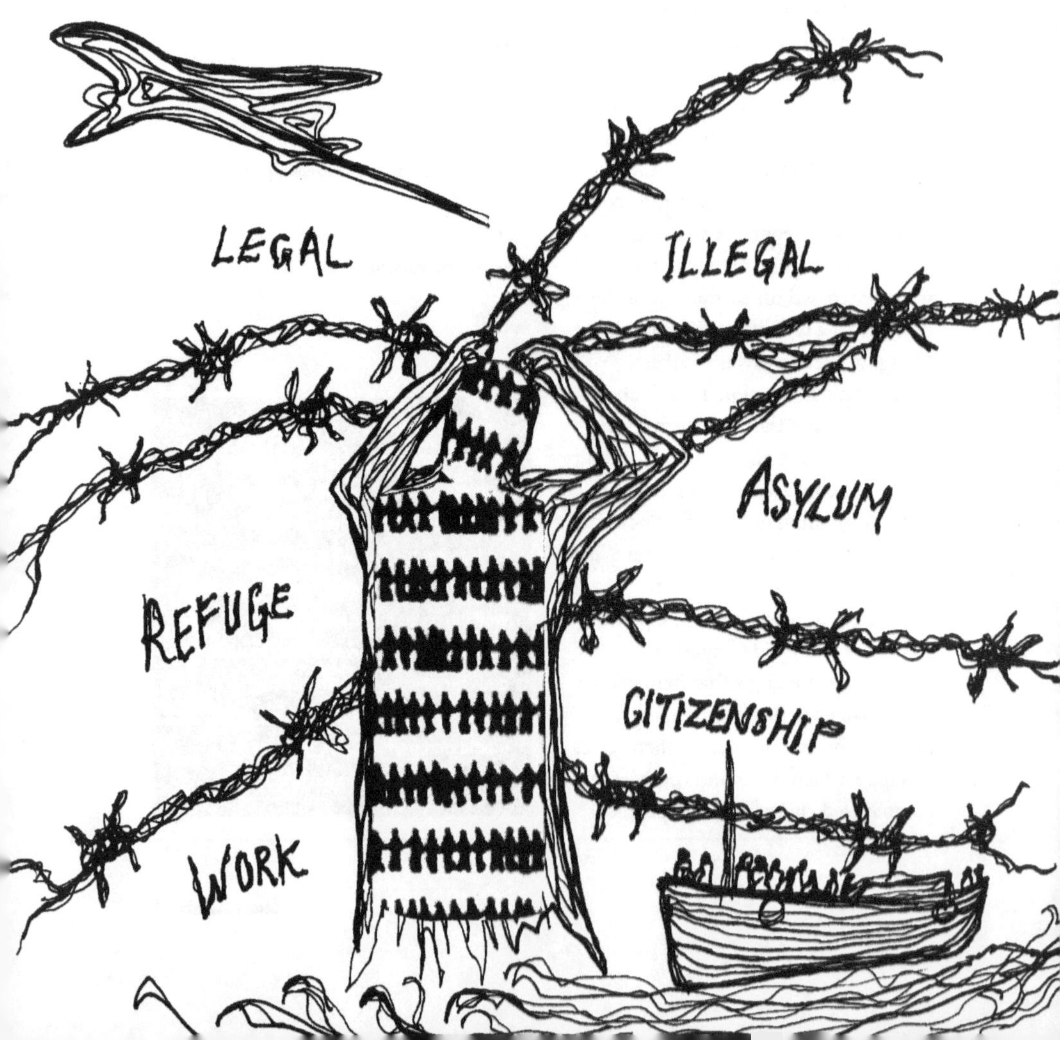

Under the guise of humanitarian work, established inter-governmental agencies like the International Organisation for Migration (IOM) and International Labour Organization (ILO) handle the enforcement of neoliberal migration management. While the IOM takes pride in being the world's largest 'human-trafficker', having moved more than 11 million people, the ILO is responsible for a 'brain-drain' of educated people from poor countries. Western governments recognise that immigrants are an additional resource for the economy since they meet the demand for cheap labour. If the demand for labour falls or their numbers exceed the demand, the immigrant workers become a burden to the state. They are then imprisoned in camps or detention centres or forcibly deported. While governments may try to maintain this situation, many undocumented migrants remain illegal to avoid the harsh detention and deportation regime.

In the UK, the official estimate for the number of 'illegal' immigrants is half a million. Many have endured a long and dangerous journey into the country. Once they are here, they end up in precarious working conditions and face increasingly strict migration laws. For many economic migrants, the options on entering Britain are limited, especially if they have entered illegally. Since asylum is not open to economic migrants, they become 'illegal' at the time of arrival without having committed any other 'crime'. However, in practical terms the distinction between legal and illegal becomes blurred as they join the legal low-waged workers in the UK. For these people there is little chance of eventually becoming legal since their existence is not recognised within the current legal framework.

It should be noted that the Labour government was recently challenged for underestimating the number of immigrants to Britain since 1997, and had to admit that most new jobs created since then went to immigrants. This admission comes at a time when economic needs are becoming a legitimate pretext for migration, to the detriment of asylum based migration for which the quota is being lowered. New Labour has proposed a new Points-Based System that will bar all but the most skilled non-EU workers [see p.40 of this issue]. A new Citizenship and Immigration Bill will set out a foreigner's duty to learn English and sign up to British values before coming into the country. Economic migration attaches conditionality to residency in new ways, with the Points-Based System further instrumentalising the role of the migrant.

The atmosphere of fear and paranoia cultivated by the state since the 9/11 and 7/7 bombings has resulted in the creation of more stringent anti-

All images by Seemab Gul

immigration laws. Recent measures involve proposals for a £1.2 billion electronic-border project and the creation of a new border agency uniting Customs and the existing Border and Immigration Service. The British government has taken steps to speed up the asylum application process resulting in an increased annual number of deportations. Asylum seekers are treated like criminals with dehumanising schemes such as electronic tagging and a voucher system trialled on them. The system by which asylum seekers bid for legal refugee status resembles a lottery, with government quotas overriding the reality of applicants' actual needs or survival chances.

Asylum seekers from war-torn countries like Sudan, Afghanistan and Iraq are sent back because these countries are considered 'safe' by a British government with deportation requirements to meet. This often comes after risking life and sacrificing savings to gain entry to the country, while the rich have student and tourist visas, 'business' options and comfortable flights available to them. Britain harnesses and safeguards rich and corrupt politicians from around the world under the pretence of 'asylum' while deporting thousands of others whose lives are seriously endangered.

For some, the decision to stay underground is not a choice but a strategy to survive the harsh climate of exclusion and fear. A legitimate application requires the asylum seeker to prove the threat they face in their country, defining them as 'guilty until proven innocent'. If the starting point is one of 'guilt' and criminality, then it can become imperative to continue this path of 'illegality'. While asylum seekers can also be economic migrants, economic migrants cannot seek asylum since 'starving' is not considered a legitimate reason for asylum. Refugees are treated as 'unfortunate, needy and honest' victims, while failed asylum seekers and economic migrants are considered liars and parasites. The Labour government insists that all 'illegals' should be deported regardless of the dangers they face in their countries of origin, but claims that it may take more than ten years to deport all 'illegals' and failed asylum seekers from the UK. The actual situation seems to be out of the government's control and is in practice regulated by the needs of the economy.

Western capitalists relocate across national boundaries and move their factories to any developing region where they can avoid taxes and exploit workers for larger profit margins. Britain, meanwhile, is slowly becoming a nation of administrators, as manual labour is increasingly undertaken by migrants. The existing working class are not only struggling for jobs and housing, but also end up having to compete with the new workers coming into their areas. Due to social and economic divisions, if it is not racism

Refugees are treated as victims, failed asylum seekers and economic migrants as liars and parasites

then it is competition that isolates the immigrants, causing further tensions.

The racist and xenophobic press has hyped the numbers of the East-European workers coming to the UK and fulminated against failed asylum seekers who protest in detention centres. The image of the 'good immigrant', i.e. hard working and law-abiding, promoted through state and mainstream media idealises middle-class immigrants. This is wielded against the majority of migrants in the UK with the intention of coercing them into the discipline of work. Despite the government's efforts to classify and tier immigrants on an individualised level, thus weakening solidarity between individuals and groups, the media stubbornly projects all immigrants as one big problem.

The influx of legal migrants from the new EU states is proof that there is a demand for low-waged workers in the UK. This demand by employers undermines the decades of struggle by British workers who have fought for the minimum wage, holiday pay and pensions. This threat is used as a stick for legal workers to stay in line or lose

out to new workers. Most new immigrants work willingly in the worst conditions and on the lowest pay because they have come a long way in search of work and survival and live in constant fear of deportation or detention. Consequently it is difficult for immigrants to demand better working conditions or to organise in the workplace, further deepening divisions between British workers and new immigrants.

To counter the ageing population in the UK and low birth rate, the liberals and the government are in agreement that there is a need for a young work force. They suggest that immigrants can and should be 'imported' to fill these gaps in the labour market. Similarly, the market demand for sex and drugs enables these industries to thrive regardless of their legal status. The desperate and 'illegal' immigrants have few options available to them but black market work.

M. Ricciardi and F. Raimondi have argued that

the point of view which aims to recognise the economic necessity of

minimum wage workers' pay after tax is often lower than those who earn cash-in-hand

migrants to contemporary social production, ultimately considers only the needs of those who offer employment and the means to satisfy these needs.[1]

Although recent migration, especially from the EU, is presenting new challenges, different ethnic groups are systematically separated, favouring those who are able to integrate well. As a result of the 'war on terror' Muslims are targeted as problem cases with more stringent visa restrictions than white Christian Eastern Europeans. The assumption that all non-Europeans must belong to a community, religion, culture or ethnicity is also an attempt to define and control immigrant populations – an attempt that underlies the integration debate. Integration may make the lives of many immigrants more tolerable but it cannot take place as long as they are ostracised as the lowest wage earners in the labour market. The integration debate is irrelevant as long as work places are divided between different 'community' groups fighting for jobs, housing and wages, with illegal workers at the bottom of the heap.

While the trade unions are losing negotiating power within the legal framework, even the legal workers are finding it hard to make demands. Ricciardi & Raimondi believe that:

migrant labour today is a condition that anticipates and shares the general conditions under which contemporary labour as a whole is distributed.[2]

Nevertheless, legal status has its benefits such as access to medical care and, in theory, housing and a greater possibility of finding work. The undocumented immigrant may aspire to civil, political and social legality, if only in the hope of improving her prospects and working conditions. Most would take up 'regularisation' or amnesty if it were offered to them in order to avoid total insecurity, the constant threat of deportation and lack of medical care. However, while hundreds of thousands may apply for amnesty in the hope of becoming legal, only a limited number will get it and then only if they fit particular criteria. The rest will be caught in a government trap having made themselves 'visible' and would face detention and deportation. Those who work in the black market might not bother with amnesty or any other legal route because they risk their livelihoods in the process.

For those who have already been detained and deported, the risks outweigh the benefits of becoming 'legal'. They have felt the violence and the bureaucracy of the state first hand, all too similar to their dealings with human traffickers. They are aware of tedious 'legal' battles with the assistance of often corrupt lawyers who try to con them out of money. The struggle to become legal almost mirrors the struggle to survive illegally. It thus becomes far easier to avoid the legal route altogether out of fear of state harassment, constant abuse and long detention before deportation.

In order to regulate the labour market, immigration regimes and border controls create 'illegals', producing their vulnerable condition once inside state borders. Making the benefits system out of bounds for undocumented migrants is therefore a safe option for the government, one that cheapens labour whilst protecting national resources. Whether the government acknowledges it or not, 'illegal immigrants' are the invisible work force within Britain. The idea of a one-off 'regularisation' or amnesty will only make a limited number of illegals into documented, regulated, taxed yet low-cost workers. While the UK government is attempting to deal with the issue of migration through a

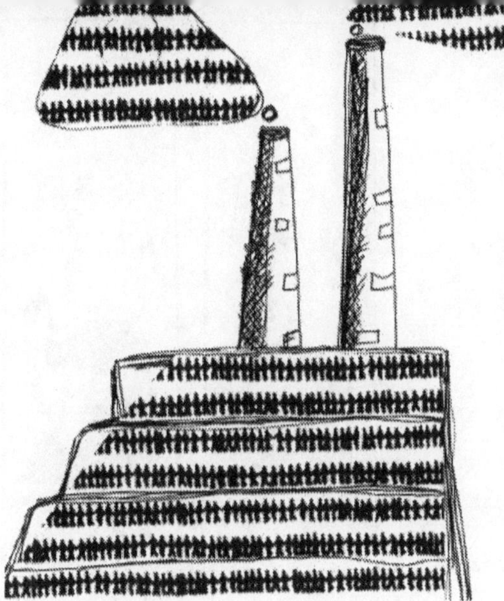

possible amnesty, borders will be sealed more tightly against future migrants - until there is a gap in the market that needs to be filled again.

Footnotes:

1 M. Ricciardi and F. Raimondi , 'Workshop IV: Migrant Labour', in *Reader for the Europe(an) Wide Preparation-Meeting of Groups, Networks and Initiatives Working on Migration* – produced for the Migrant Labour conference, held at Queen Mary College, London, 2004.

2 Ibid.

Links:

http://www.noii.org.uk
http://www.noborder.org
http://thistuesday.org
http://www.migreurop.org

Seemab Gul <sab76@mail.com> works at Mute magazine and supports London No Borders. Her multi-media works span themes of migration, identity, culture and politics

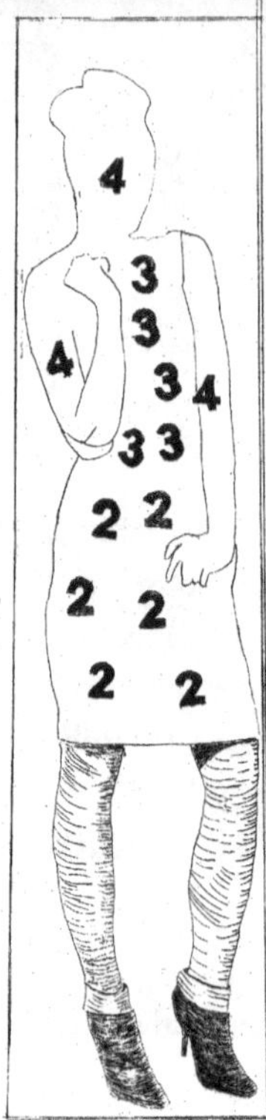

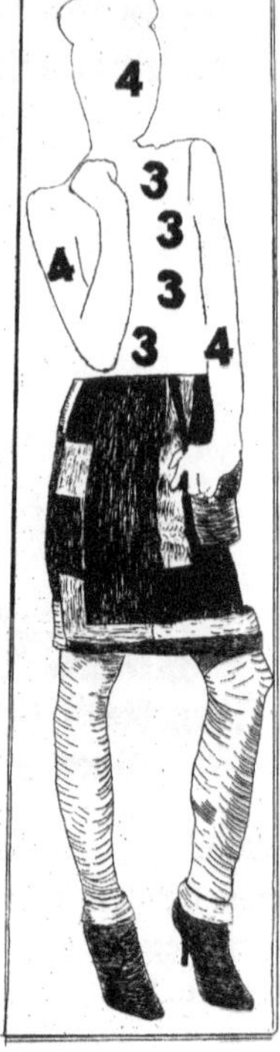

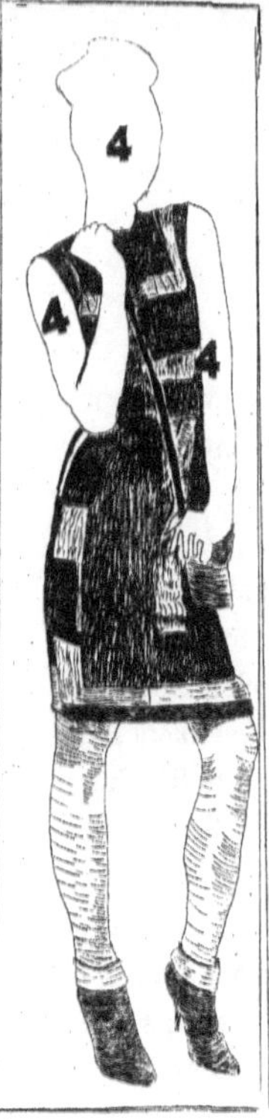

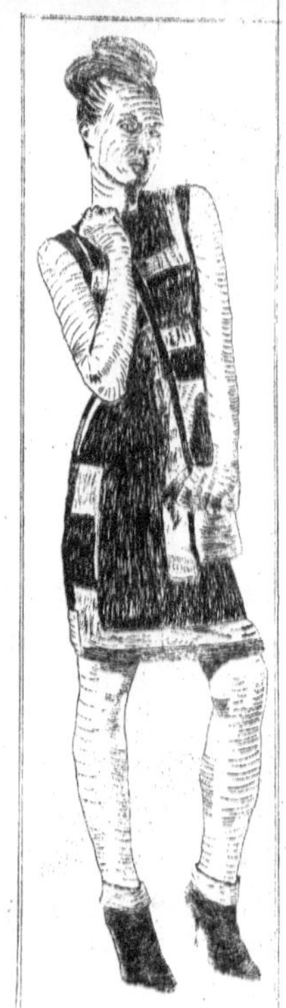

POINTS-BASED PEONAGE

All immigrants are equal, but some are more equal than others. The introduction of a points-based immigration system in the UK will intensify workers' vulnerability to the state and employers, reports Javier

The new Points-Based System (PBS), will gradually come into force in 2008. According to the Home Office, the starting point is that employers should look first to recruit from the UK and the expanded EU before recruiting migrants from outside the EU. The latter are allocated points depending on their 'benefit to the UK' and will all have to fit into one of five tiers which, in turn, determines what rights they are entitled to during their stay. Most non-EU migrants will need a sponsor – business or educational institution – to come into the country.

The Five Tier Hierarchy:

Tier 1 – Highly Skilled Migrants

Similar to existing schemes to attract 'the best and brightest' of migrants that will 'increase the productivity and growth of the UK economy'. They will be able to bring their families and allowed to settle after a further two years of testing. They are the only group that do not need a sponsor.

Tier 2 – Skilled workers with job offer

It is expected that this will be the route for most arrivals. This tier is basically employers recruiting overseas, either for jobs identified as suffering a shortage of labour, or after proving that the new arrival is not displacing a UK or EU potential worker. For example, the employer may have to show it will pay a competitive salary that will not undercut average wages for the job. Tier 2 migrants will be allowed to bring dependants and settle after five years. They can change employer and even move to Tier 1, but will have to go through a re-assessment by the Home Office.

Tier 3 – Low skilled migration

These are the migrants who will suffer the worst restrictions. The Home Office's five year plan is to 'phase out' schemes for impoverished non-EU migrants. Again, recruitment of overseas workers will be limited to sectors with a shortage of labour, where cheap EU workers cannot be recruited, and only from countries that sign a 'returns arrangement' with the UK. These workers will only be allowed into the UK for a maximum of a year, without families, and they will not be allowed to switch to other tiers. Options considered to ensure workers return at the end of their leave include bonds, compulsory remittances, open return tickets and biometric capture.

Tier 4 – Students

The main change here is the greater responsibility for educational institutions to police immigration compliance. Students will be allowed to change courses but not institutions without a fresh claim, and will be allowed to bring in their family. Current UK working regulations remain unchanged for this category.

Tier 5 – Youth mobility and temporary workers

This is a rag-bag of schemes for people coming to the UK mainly 'to satisfy non-economic objectives'. Au pairs, artists, volunteers for charity, etc. will fall in the Temporary Workers category. They will be allowed a maximum stay of 24 months without

Images by Lee Galpin

Show Invisibles?

the possibility of changing tiers, and will be allowed to bring dependants. Youth mobility schemes will be set up with specific countries that act as sponsors vouching for their youngsters' return. Countries will be rated, quotas and even bans will be imposed 'according to immigration risk'. This scheme will cover people aged 18-30, who are allowed a maximum of 24 months, no family and no change of tier.

How Points Work

Points are meant to provide a structured and objective decision making process so infallible that the right of appeal will be replaced by administrative review.

Points are awarded for:

– Attributes: qualifications (bonus to have a UK education), previous earnings (relative to local economy), work history, age (to compensate for lower youth earnings), English language (compulsory for Tiers 1 and 2).
– Control factors: Certificate of Sponsorship, funds, history of compliance with migration controls.

There are great variations on how points work for each tier and we do not have the space here to fully explain it. The system is designed for a trade off in points, but a central part is the Certificate of Sponsorship.

Sponsorship:

The main radical departure from the existing migration model is the outsourcing of migration controls, and associated costs and responsibilities, from the Home Office towards those perceived as 'benefiting from migration'. The PBS converts employers and educational institutions into sponsors, who must select the right migrants – both in skills and compliance – make sure they follow their stated role and that they leave in due time. Sponsors 'will be expected to report any prolonged absence from work or discontinuation of studies'.

All sponsors will have to be approved by the Home Office, who will rate them as A or B depending on their 'track record and policies'. A-rated sponsors will always bring in good migrants and get their paperwork right, etc. According to the Home Office, they

> can expect that the applications from the migrants they sponsor will generally be successful... and a light touch from us.

Resources thus will focus on policing B-rated sponsors and their migrants.

It is obvious how this will save time and money at the Home Office, but it is equally clear that this leaves workers in an incredibly vulnerable position in relation to their employers. The words 'bonded labour' come to mind. The first casualty of the sponsor system will be imported domestic workers. After endless cases of maids being beaten, imprisoned, deprived of their documents and generally treated like modern slaves, the government agreed some years ago that it might be a good idea to let them look for alternative employers. Alas, with the PBS they will be once again tied to their sponsor, come rain or shine.

What It All Means

In fact the PBS will directly affect a relatively small number of those coming into this country in a vulnerable position. It is mainly a repackaging of existing schemes, where the devil will be in the detail of how points are allocated, the assessment of perceived labour shortages and the issues with sponsors mentioned above.

The big problems with the PBS lie elsewhere. It further reduces migration policy to a one-way street of 'benefit to UK' that does not take into account the realities of both globalisation and human aspirations. The assumption is that migrants are informed individuals making cost-benefit decisions that match the cold calculations of the government on how many hands, divided by two, we must import to keep inflation at bay. Chance, poverty, love, war, family ties, repression, rumours, etc. do not win you any points here.

The alternative for most migrants will be more of the same: hyper-exploitation in illegal work or the destitution of asylum.

We also need to see how the PBS will impact all migrants. The stated focus on the UK and EU first could easily be understood by many as government sanctioned racist discrimination against non-whites. The three quarters of a million people trapped in the current system, both visa over-stayers and legacy asylum cases, are simply ignored in the PBS plan.

Finally, the implementation of the PBS depends on the development of a comprehensive electronic control apparatus. Basically a 'management information system' that will keep track of every migrant entering, staying in, and leaving the UK, producing patterns of non-compliance for migrants from particular countries and job sectors. This in turn will only be possible with biometric controls and ID, not just for migrants but for everyone, as one cannot make racist assumptions on who is and who is not a UK citizen.

This text is based on 'The Points-Based Immigration System: Making Migrants Work for Britain',
http://www.indymedia.org.uk/en/2007/04/369098.html

NO ONE IS LEGAL

Where the struggle for migrants' rights can be risky and divisive, informal organising by 'illegals' is a means to ensure survival. But both formal and informal organising can combine to protect an essential buffer zone of invisibility for undocumented workers — writes <u>Unterschreber</u>

The delirious belief that 'Britain has lost control of its borders' has been affirmed repeatedly of late by Citizens, i.e. those people well enough served by the current border control regime to be able to imagine they have an interest in its survival. In reality, however, the spread of this hallucination more or less coincides with the build up of the most severe restrictions ever imposed on non-European foreigners' freedom to enter and stay in the country.[1] The Points-Based System due to come into force next year will tighten criteria even further, while 'democratising' border policing by legally obliging Citizens to act as informers [see Javier, 'Points-Based Peonage', page 42 of this issue].

The leaky border is by no means just a 'tabloid' (middleclass-brow slang for 'dumb prole') fancy. It is perpetuated, for instance, in generally well-informed, sceptical publications as divergent ideologically as *Lobster* and *Private Eye*. Thus even the 'critical' elements within the expert commentator classes betray total obliviousness to the everyday reality of immigration policing that surrounds them; an ignorance compounded by a sorry failure of imagination. Not only have the pundits themselves evidently never had to cross the UK or Schengen borders, much less tried to live and work, without the privileges of Euro-nationality; it would seem that nothing in the life experience of the sheltered social circles they move in gives them any clue either.[2] (As a corrective, I suggest a simple comparative experiment: travel between London and Paris by Eurostar one way and Megabus the other, and watch the border guards at work.)

Perhaps such disconnection from reality is not so surprising on the part of those inside the gilded cocoon that Pasolini called 'the Palazzo'. What really is impressive, though, is that in spite of the unprecedented apparatus of prohibition and enforcement in place, plus the constant flow of ex-entrants back out of the country, enough new non-'Europeans' get through at all to maintain any kind of collective presence, much less serve as a pretext for racist panic.[3] Silvia Federici wrote in 1990 of the apparent contradiction

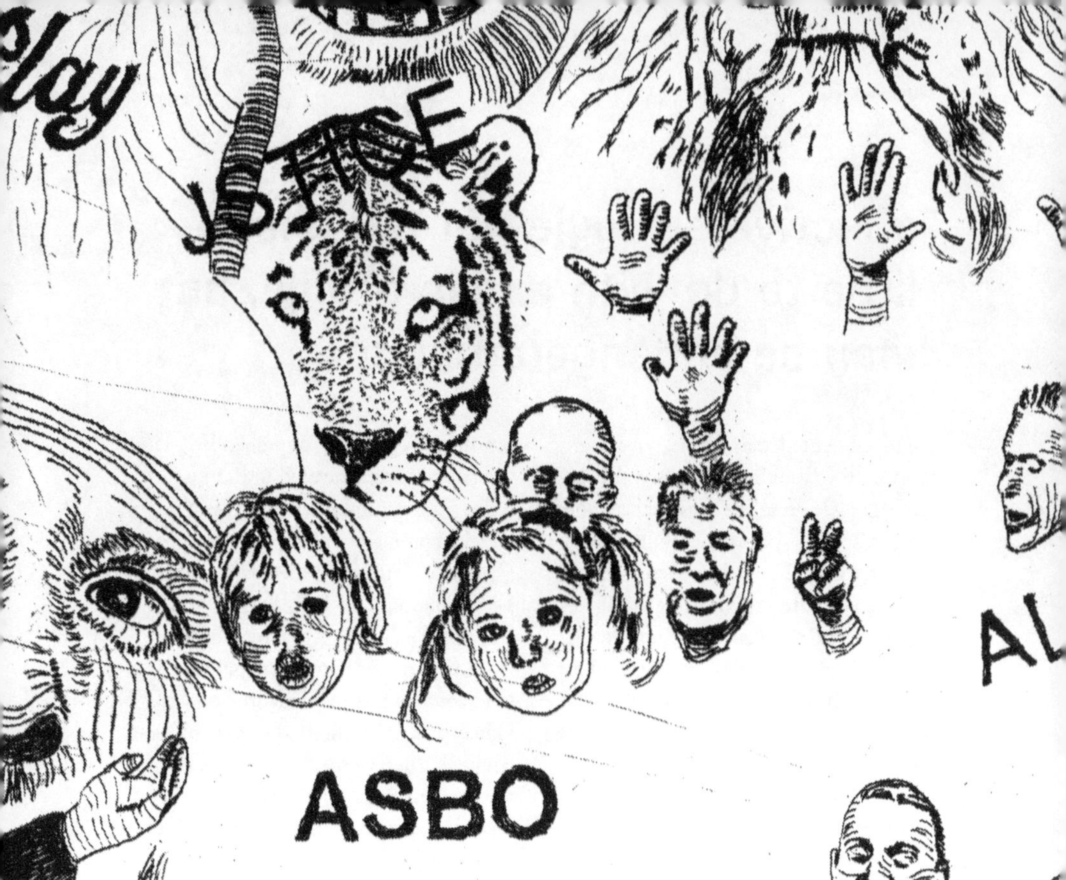

by which, 'according to the statistics gathered by international agencies, most people in Africa ought to be dead, since their income per capita is far below subsistence', whereas the 'dark' continent is actually 'one of the liveliest places on the planet'.[4] The reason for the pseudo-paradox, of course, lay in the resilience of collective 'informal' reproduction practices that don't register in computer models, and which the headquarters of statistically viable 'economic activity' have not ceased trying to stamp out. Or in other words, physical, intellectual and social struggle, which may or may not be acknowledged as 'political'.

A superficially similar logic can be seen at work in Britain and the other wings of the European fortress inasmuch as, legally and statistically speaking, it's 'impossible' for most migrants to be here, especially without displaying signs of the pitiful dependency entailed by 'asylum seeker' status (whether in formal detention or its annex, the voucher queue). Yet, as the result of intense struggle, there they are, in living spite of demographic measure, and by no means helplessly entrusting life or death to state or NGO decision or activist advocacy. Once again, it comes down to the effectiveness of 'informal' social mechanisms which not only do not court 'rights', but actively confound visibility, let alone representation.

To acknowledge the function of this

   All images by Lee Galpin   **Show Invisibles?**

effective struggle not only has little to do with public profile, but may be endangered by it

undocumented action does not mean celebrating it indiscriminately: the rate of exploitation in the informal economy organised on 'community' lines is well-known, as is the smooth incorporation of the absolute surplus value pumped from it into the same 'legitimate' capitalism which, without the slightest contradiction, also demands aggressive border controls. But the struggle going on at this level, and its position in the 'wider economy' is central to the questions that need to be answered for the meaning of any programme of 'organising around illegality' to be clear.

One organised group of migrants struck an illegal, physical blow for collective freedom on 4 August this year by breaking out of Campsfield immigration prison in Oxfordshire at the end of a mass hunger strike.[5] The No Border Network quickly responded with solidarity demonstrations at immigration 'reporting' (i.e. surrendering to potential detention and deportation) centres across the country.[6] Meanwhile Imam Dr. Abduljalil Sajid, ex-chairman of the Joint Council for the Welfare of Immigrants, advised the escapees to give themselves up.[7] In general, though, the historic breach of internment was reported as an ordinary police incident. The BBC gave star billing to one Bill Smith, who privately 'apprehended', imprisoned and delivered to the militarised manhunt a fugitive who knocked on his door 'begging for assistance'. The story 'died' when 11 (or 14, depending on which account you read) of the 26 escapees remained at large after their photos were published to encourage further vigilante kidnappings. The limited success of the jailbreak, then, is measured by, or at least corresponds to, its sustained disappearance from 'the public eye' (i.e. representation in bourgeois media and competitive politics), rather than by any visibility as advertisement for the 'rights' requested by Imam Sajid.

The use of such direct methods in unrepresented struggle by rightless *extracomunitari* is the theme of *Evasioni e rivolte* (*Escapes and Rebellions*)[8], a new book by robustly contested *Mute* contributor Emilio Quadrelli.[9] It mostly consists of interviews with escapees from Italian immigration prisons ('CPT', literally 'centres of temporary permanence'). Quadrelli quotes statistics indicating a shift since mid-2005 in detainees' response to conditions, with individual self-mutilation, petty gangsterism and violence between nationally aligned prisoner factions tending to be replaced by violence co-ordinated across

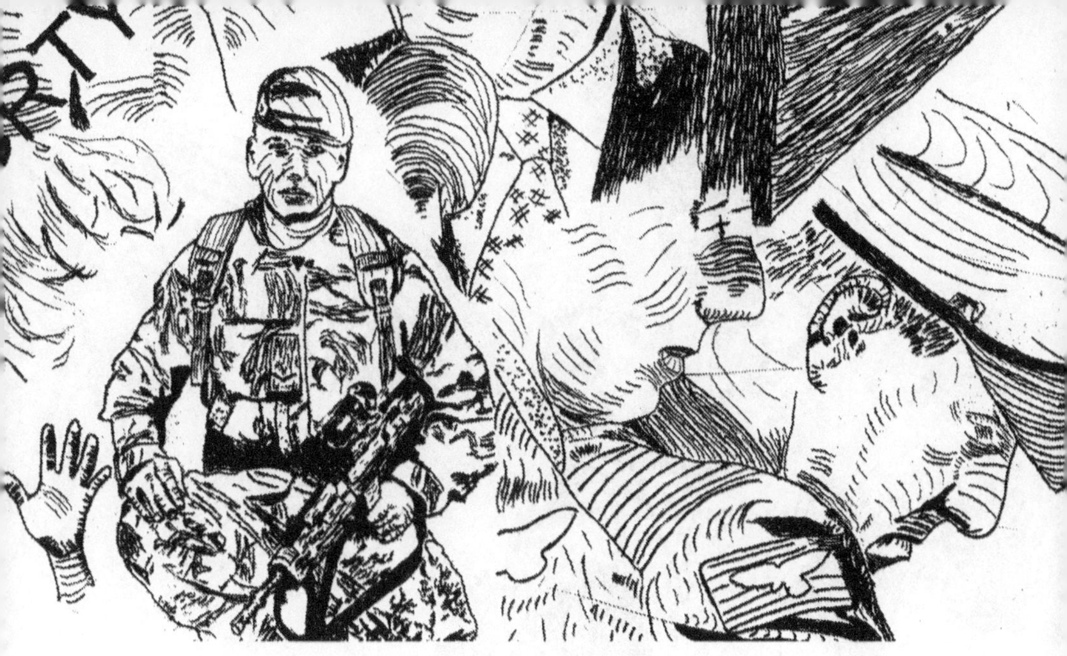

nationality lines against the institutions and their guards, sometimes leading to collectively planned escape.[10]

The book works as a polemic against the image of illegal immigrants as tragic victims, but the point is not to fetishise escape from detention. Rather, the CPT episodes are restored to the context of the speakers' experience as migrant workers, with 'work' understood to include all varieties of formal, informal, semi-legal and 'criminal' employment, whether in regular industrial, casual, domestic or opportunistic street settings. Thus the stories can be said to be 'about' the use in labour discipline of 'illegality' and of racial stratification between 'illegals', and the comparative effectiveness of different tactics of resistance, flight or counter-attack. Particular emphasis is placed on the role of immigrant 'community leaders' and public spokesmen in managing the flow of business between 'official' and 'illegal' economies, reproducing class hierarchy both within the 'communities' and between them on an overall social level. (For example a Moroccan factory owner 'sponsors' extended family members' legal entry into Italy then withholds their visas, effectively indenturing their labour in his sweatshop unless they wish to fall into the hands of his paid-off local police. Or Roma elders periodically 'sell' younger travellers into the CPT in a deal with the city council to postpone demolition of their site.)[11] In one story after another, capture and CPT internment results from various kinds of bosses' reaction to the migrants' semi-organised attempts at resistance. Then, with remarkable regularity, after initial helplessness and despair the detainees refine their co-operation and planning and extend it beyond single 'ethnic community' lines, thereby attaining relative power within the CPT and eventually escaping. They generally end by saying they have survived within illegality 'on their own

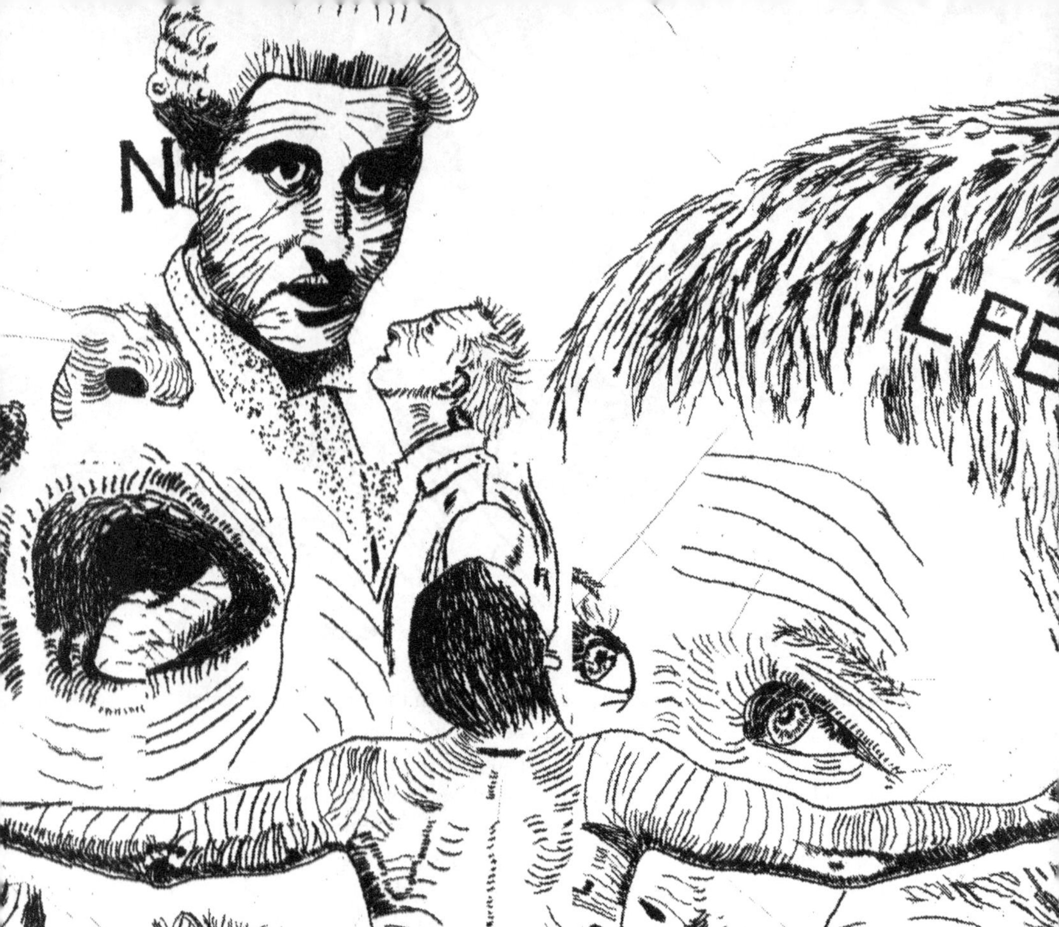

terms' since escape thanks to the same forms of small group self-organisation and carefully circumscribed violence that got them out of the prison.

Claims like these for something like collective self-sufficiency 'outside the system' are highly dubious, of course especially where the same speakers have eloquently described the integration into 'legitimate' capital of the 'criminal' economic circuits which now apparently support their independence. But then the narrators' reasons for preferring prudent self-mythologising to factual detail when talking about their present lives are also not hard to imagine. The extravagant 'military' feats that occur in the stories even before they reach 'happy' open-endings may or may not have been substituted for compromising 'realistic' detail. What certainly is realistic, however, is the speakers' suspicion that effective struggle not only has little to do with public profile, but may actually be endangered by it; their awareness that what amounts to invisibilty from certain points of view may be essential to struggle's practical success.

Any attempt to 'organise around illegality', then, would perhaps have to bear these points in mind. Yet it's hard to see how it would be possible to do so where the struggle revolves around 'rights' (e.g. to trade union representation). 'Rights within illegality' remains an oxymoron however far the terms are stretched, because 'rights', by definition, must be legislated into existence and the law publicly enforced, otherwise they're merely slogans that call for something on uncertain grounds without obtaining it in practice. To raise this problem is not just semantic nit-picking: unfortunately it's all too easy to imagine the unintended (by sincere campaigners at least) effects that could arise if limited legal rights were granted, under trade union tutelage, to some 'illegal' workers within a framework that ultimately maintained their 'illegal immigrant' status. The workers concerned would still not have obtained the full freedom of movement, association and withdrawal of labour that they'd need in order to respond to bosses' blackmail with independent counter-coercion, whether collectively or individually. Yet the new legal rights would be sure to entail legal responsibilities, probably forcing the workers to become institutionally visible and thereby to lose the last resort option of disappearance from intolerable work situations and from the immigration police, whose powers over them would remain. In fact a situation like this might even increase dependency and stratification within the lowest, most exploited labour strata. The 'lucky' semi-semi-legals would acquire a new sponsor/overseer in the union, outside whose umbrella they'd

'Rights within illegality' remains an oxymoron

fall back into supposed helplessness. Meanwhile a new hierarchical division could arise between this group and those who are still simply illegal, stimulating yet more of the desperate competition between workers that the whole system is designed to cultivate.

However these problems with 'union rights' as a campaign goal, and the habit of measuring immigrants' willingness to struggle by their union participation, certainly don't mean action by workers organised in unions must always be useless or counter-productive. In summer this year the rank and file members of Finsbury Park RMT called for a union conference against immigration control, following a similar event held in Liverpool in March.[12] The proposed agenda contained the germ of a radically different approach. Topics included: 'how do we stop migrants being singled out by employers to produce papers?', and 'defiance not compliance', i.e. organising refusal to participate in reporting on 'illegals', cutting off their benefits and deporting them. 'Non-cooperation' with immigration control by workers higher in the labour hierarchy created through the same controls will become more crucial than ever as the state moves to devolve responsibility for enforcement onto employers, whose 'legal' employees will in turn be expected to do the dirty work of monitoring and informing. This strategy also contrasts with that of campaigning for 'rights' in that, under the new law, the non-cooperating workers would be entering into illegality themselves rather than trying to use their privileges on behalf of the vulnerable. This could constitute a significant step towards ending the isolation of 'illegals'. It would also help workers prepare to defend themselves against the conditions they face when the 'database state', which union campaigners rightly point out is initially for use in immigration/labour policing, is extended to attack the scraps of freedom and income 'illegally' enjoyed by the wider working class.[13]

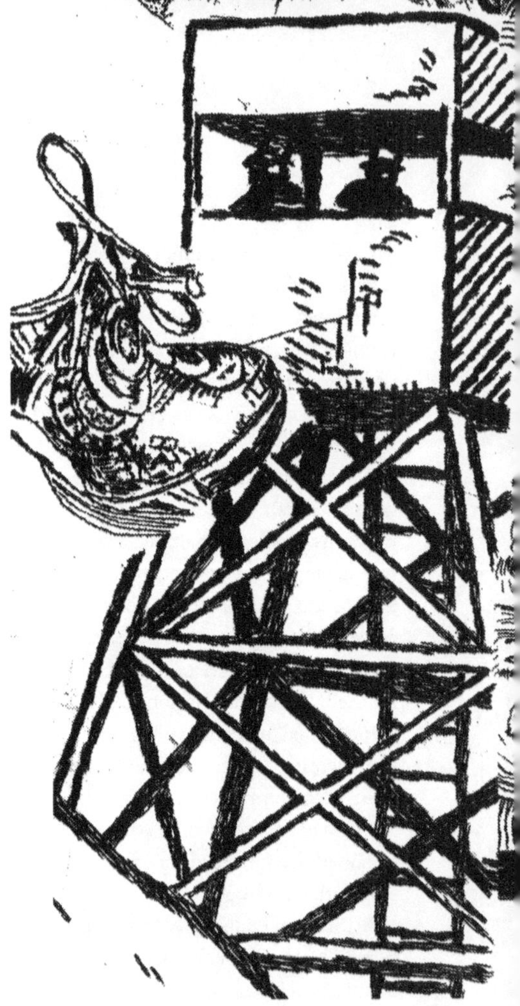

Footnotes

1 Strictly speaking, non-EU by citizenship and non-British, French, Italian etc. by ancestry. When the UK first introduced immigration controls in the 1960s, the legislation was framed so as to let in the children and some grandchildren of British settlers in the former colonies, but not the bloody natives. Hence, for example, the colour and class of the majority of self-proclaimed 'escapees' in Britain from 'pariah states' like South Africa in the 1960s-'70s-'80s or Zimbabwe today. These racist provisions substantially remain in place.

2 The indignation of many Europeans at the 9/11 travel restrictions in the US bespeaks habituation to fast-tracking privileges in the EU, with an ensuing blindness to Europe's 'American-style' processing of everyone else.

3 'Non-European' in the sense explained in footnote 1. For the sake of brevity, henceforth simply 'migrants' unless otherwise stated. 'Borders-out-of-control' hysterics, incidentally, might claim in their own defence that they weren't just talking

about 'non-Europeans' but about overall numbers.
But they almost never call for the French, Germans
or British-ancestry New Zealanders to be kicked
out, and they rarely even pose the 'problem' as one
of EU expansion as such, at least since it actually
happened. Rather, they demand that border
repression, which under the law as it stands targets
non-'Europeans' exclusively and with
unprecedented force, be made even more aggressive
than it already is.

Once comprehensively defeated on all statistical
and material grounds, opponents of immigration
eventually whimper about 'social cohesion' being
under threat. At this point they reveal more about
their 'core beliefs' than they probably intended:
'social cohesion' based on nationality is a racist
fantasy, and if it ever existed more concretely
anywhere it would need to be destroyed by any
means available. See also: http://www.spiked-
online.com/index.php?/behmnr/article/4030/

4 Silvia Federici, 'The Debt Crisis, Africa & the
New Enclosures', *Midnight Notes* 10, p.15.

5 See:
http://www.indymedia.org.uk/en/2007/08/377991.html

6 See 'They all belong to Glasgow', interview with
Ahmed Kahn, *Variant* 25, for an idea of the threat
to physical security faced by troublemakers at these
sites.
http://www.variant.randomstate.org/25texts/brand25.html

7 The phrase 'give yourself up' can rarely have
corresponded any more precisely to the actual
stakes of surrender. See:
http://news.bbc.co.uk/1/hi/england/oxfordshire/693
2553.stm

8 Emilio Quadrelli, Evasioni e rivolte, Milan:
Agenzia X, 2007.
http://www.agenziax.it/?pid=13&sid=30

9 See: http://www.metamute.org/en/Terraces-and-
Peripheries;
http://www.metamute.org/en/Grassroots-political-
militants-Banlieusards-and-politics;
http://www.metamute.org/en/French-Banlieues-
and-Urban-Guerrillas

10 Quadrelli, pages 10-12. The list of incidents
ends in November 2005, but CPT riots and mass
escapes have continued to be reported regularly in
mainstream Italian media, with little attempt to
portray the events as unusual or surprising. No
comparable shift in detainees' response to
detention has been reported in Britain, because
prisoner revolt has barely ceased here since the
'facilities' were opened. Group escape during
rioting has been less common, though not
unknown.

11 Visa sponsorship is about to return to the UK,
thanks once again to the Points-Based System. For
more on the implications *see*: Javier, 'Points-Based
Peonage', *Mute* Vol 2 #7, originally published at
http://www.indymedia.org.uk/en/2007/04/369098.html

12 See:
http://noborderslondon.blogspot.com/2007/07/uni
on-conference-against-immigration.html

13 See the text cited in footnote 11.

> **Any resemblance between persons living
> or dead and Unterschreber is entirely
> deplorable**

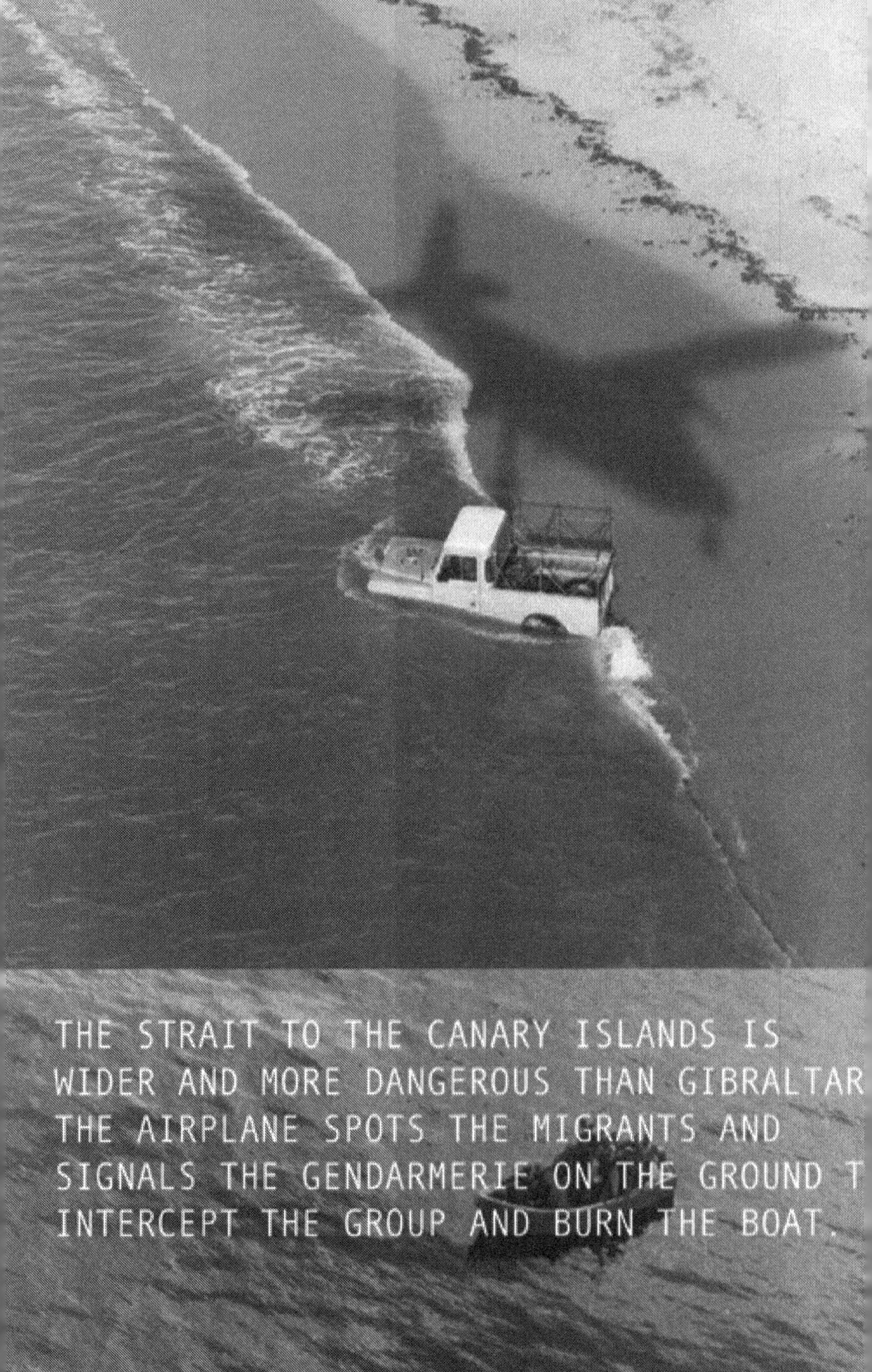
THE STRAIT TO THE CANARY ISLANDS IS
WIDER AND MORE DANGEROUS THAN GIBRALTAR
THE AIRPLANE SPOTS THE MIGRANTS AND
SIGNALS THE GENDARMERIE ON THE GROUND T
INTERCEPT THE GROUP AND BURN THE BOAT.

VISUALISING INVISIBILITY

The Arnolfini's show Port City: On Mobility and Exchange deals with the conflicts between illegal migrants' need to remain invisible and art's necessity to reveal what is hidden. Review by <u>Jennifer Thatcher</u>

In a recent lecture at the ICA (26 October 2007) on the futile rhetoric of resistance, Slavoj Žižek criticised the ineffectiveness of political anarchism, the fashionable strategy championed by academics and activists who levy attacks on governments from the sidelines. Such activists, he argues, operate safe in the knowledge that, in the case of anti-war demonstrations for example, their actions will not affect policy, and furthermore that the tedious, bureaucratic business of governing their nation will continue unaffected. On the dirty issue of immigration, Žižek scorned the naivety of a liberal open-door policy, and played up the paradoxical situation of anarchists helping immigrants to gain state-recognised status. But Žižek proposed no miracle solution: if he was defending the principle of democracy and the need to extend political participation and rights to those who are currently unrepresented, he was disdainful of current mainstream representational politics, and particularly Third Way solutions. Nonetheless, it's not hard to imagine, given his logic, what he might have thought of the touring exhibition on migration initiated by Bristol's Arnolfini gallery: another attempt to assuage the liberal conscience.

However, if the art gallery remains, in this country at least, a safe ghetto for radical musings on contemporary politics, it is wrong to dismiss all art, and indeed culture for that matter, as entirely frivolous, despite its frequently tokenistic and clumsy attempts to appear concerned. Liam Gillick, in his blog relating to the Memorial to the Iraq War exhibition, also at the ICA earlier this year, pointed to the need for artists, in unacceptably dire political times, to 'step outside their normal practice' and make their objections known as citizens foremost. But to separate the responsibilities of creativity from those of citizens does a dangerous disservice to the potentials of art, forcing art to retreat into mere entertainment and severing its link with the world around it. Port City is an ideal case study through which to observe the relationship between the political concerns of artists and their artistic expression.

Gillick does go on, nevertheless, to

Image: Still from Sahara Chronicle, Ursual Biemann, 2006-7

Show Invsibles?

propose a useful function of art, as a marker and multiplier of differences and as 'a perfect form for the revelation of paradox'. And artist-curator Ursula Biemann's major contribution to Port City – in the form of photographs, documentary videos, commissioned film programme and eloquent catalogue essay – persuasively demonstrates the value of presenting different voices. Taking up the whole ground floor gallery at the Arnolfini, her crowded video installation *Sahara Chronicle* (2006-7) established the Maghreb (Morocco, Algeria, Libya, Tunisia) as the focal point for the exhibition's exploration of issues surrounding displacement and migration,

particularly following the Schengen Agreement that, since the mid-1980s, has sanctioned free movement across most of Europe at the expense of tightening both its borders with North Africa and, as a cruel knock-on effect, dismantling the latter's own internal 'open-door' policy.

Her video interviews map the scale of the migratory network in sub-Saharan Africa: the diverse provenance of those intent on moving ever northwards to Morocco and eventually Europe to seek jobs and fortune for their families; the parasitic entrepreneurs, from the 'coxer' or broker who takes commission for arranging migrants' travel to the next

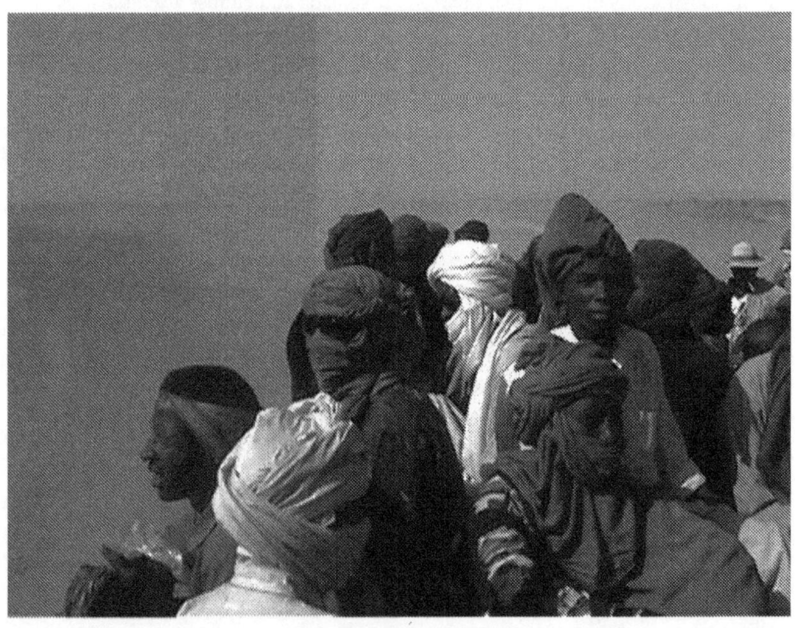

Image: Still from Sahara Chronicle, Ursual Biemann, 2006-7

Liam Gillick pointed to the need for artists to 'step outside their normal practice' and make their objections known as citizens

border, to the 'production manager' filling out forms and taking fees, and the drivers of the Sahara Transport Company's monstrous 4x4s with headlamps literally at human head height. Harrowing interviews with interned clandestines defy any romantic notion of a symbiotic relationship between these self-proclaimed 'brothers': these particular migrants gave themselves up to the police following four days' starvation and dehydration at the hands of their guides. This is bare life.

Roving surveillance cameras are the vicarious eyes of the authorities, listlessly watching over the vast Saharan desert for signs of life. The stream-of-consciousness style of much of the footage increases the palpability of the endless waits; the days, even months of being on the road – and, by extension, the sense of hope that seeks to override the very real anticipation of being caught. By contrast, the shorter looped film sequences mirror the cyclical nature of these transactions, whereby the same transport company is employed by the authorities to return unsuccessful migrants as the one which brought them to the border. Biemann describes this approach to filming as

'sustainable representation', not simply in opposition to the geological issues of desertification that face the region, but also as a conscious alternative to the 'targeted shots' of mainstream news reporting that fix their subjects as stereotypes, denying their potentiality to take on other, less newsworthy roles.

This complex web of relationships between migrant, broker and the authorities underlines the inadequacy of the binary models with which we are usually confronted by the media: victim/perpetrator; legal/illegal. Biemann leaves us in no doubt as to the geopolitical roots of this psychical complexity. The brokers are ex-Tuareg rebels, who, returning to their capital Agadez in Niger after the rebellion of the early 1990s, set up the transport business for lack of other employment opportunities; the authorities are able to keep a level of control over this semi-legal operation, aware that it keeps the rebels in a compromised position over their own semi-legal citizenship.

The central Saharan Tuareg territory itself was split between five countries in a colonial agreement in 1884, which has left this nomadic tribe a minority in their host nations. The French built a uranium mine at Arlit in

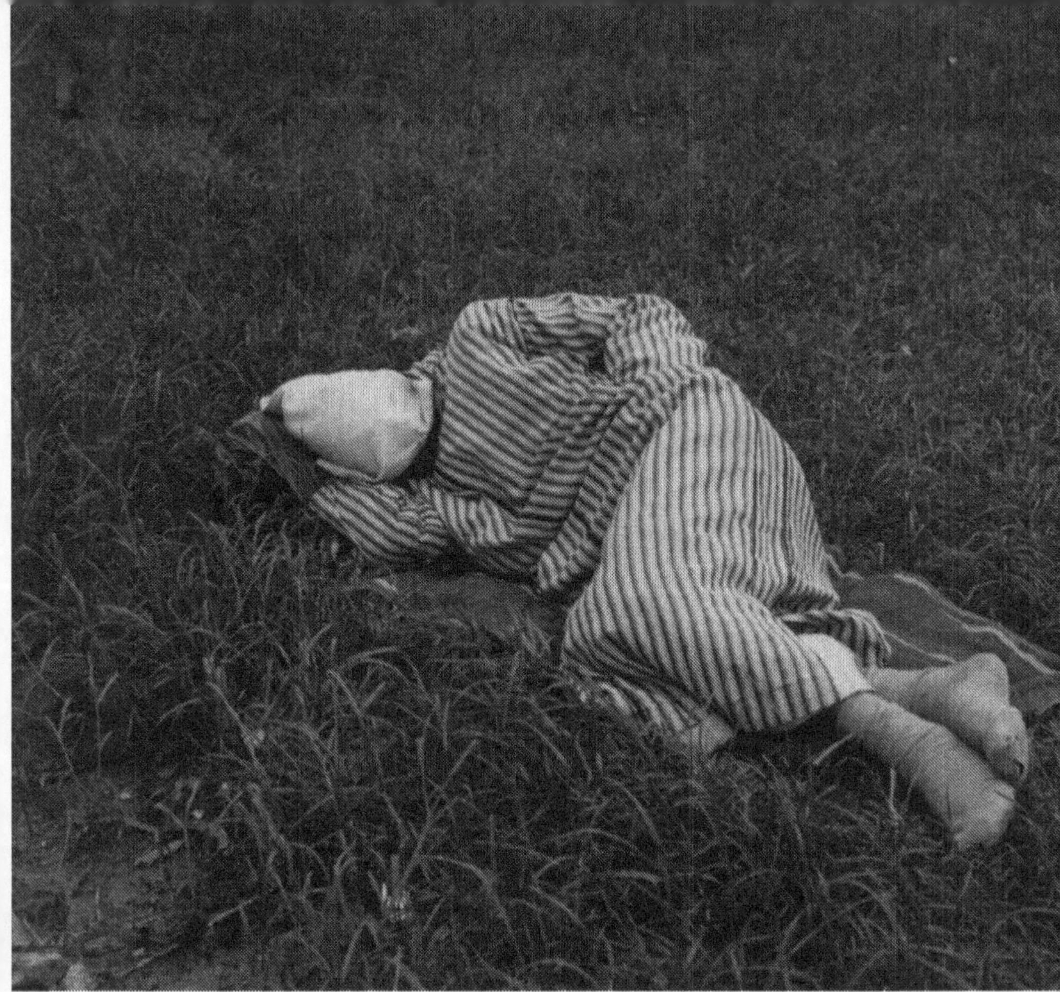

Niger during the Cold War, largely eschewing the Tuareg for their own, foreign workforce; at the end of the Cold War, uranium from the new markets caused prices, and employment numbers, to plummet. The Tuareg, then as now, and like so many native tribes, have lost badly at the hands of the colonialists. Paradoxically, the Tuareg Diaspora has recently grown in importance as the tribe's knowledge of the terrain and links across borders can be exploited for the clandestine migration business; Biemann describes the Tuareg as the 'hyphen' between the poorer Suhal zone (Mali, Chad, Niger) and the Arab North.

While Biemann is sensitive to the moral dilemma in making visible those who necessarily strive to remain invisible, she nonetheless perceives the process of bringing buried truths to light as an important function of contemporary art. Yto Barrada's voyeuristic suite of black-and-white photographs, *Sleepers 1-3* (2006), zoom in on the awkward figures of men sleeping on patches of grass. Lying face down on the ground or covered by a makeshift hood, these men protect

Images: From the series Sleepers 1-3, Yto Barada, 2006

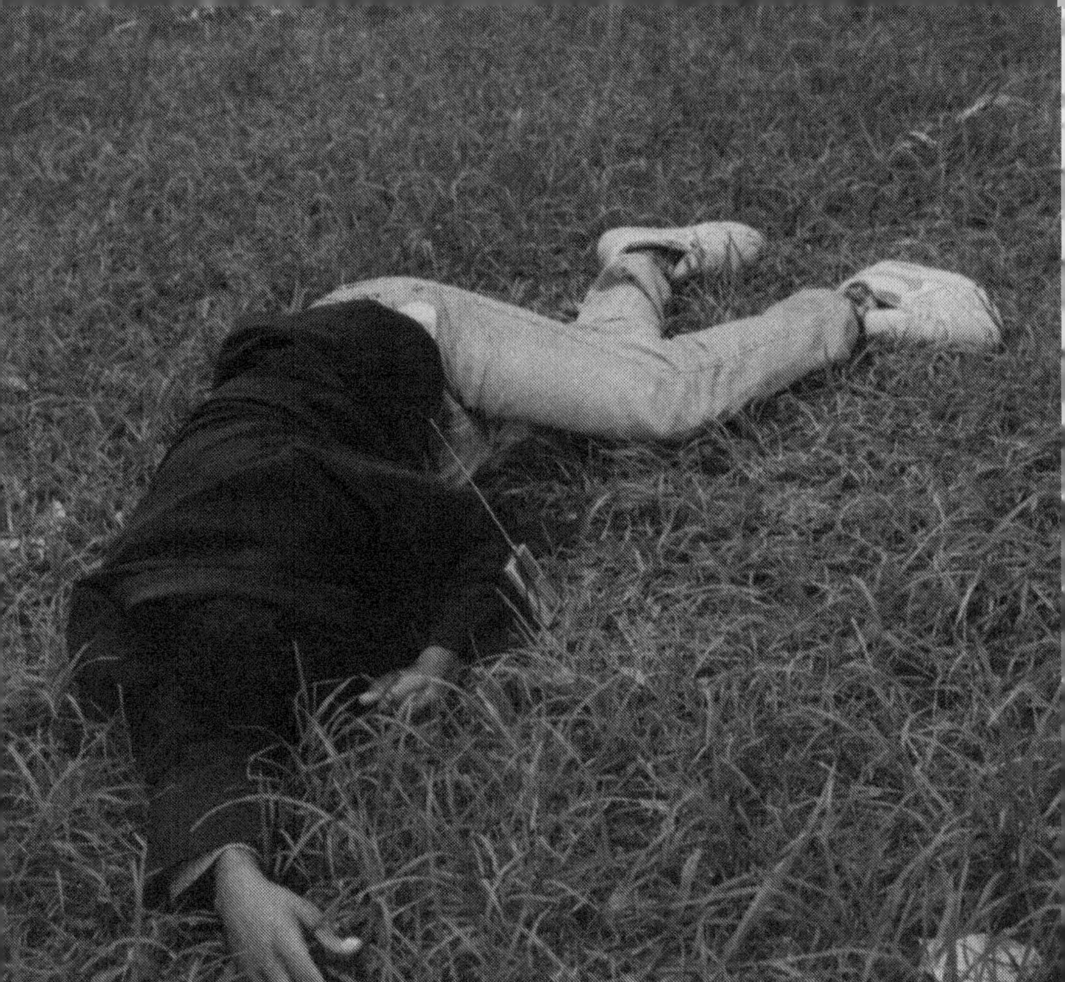

their faces against the blinding sun of Tangier, but also from the judgement of our gazes. Their physical anonymity echoes their legal status as the 'burnt ones': those who destroy their identity papers and with it the evidence of their past in preparation for the attempted illegal crossing to Spain – tantalisingly beckoning across the Gibraltar Strait. Their mummified stillness is an all-too-real portent of the deadly risks involved in crossing the Strait that Arnolfini director Tom Trevor has called 'a vast Moroccan cemetery'. Yet these photographs restore a level of dignity to these men: highlighting their plight without compromising their identity. Zineb Sedira likewise dramatises the growing isolation of Algeria from Europe, as the protagonists in her wistful and formally elegant two-screen film *Saphir* (2006) – a young man and the middle-aged pied-noir owner of a deserted colonial hotel – stare out to sea across the handsome but neglected port of Algiers, with ambiguous expressions that might be variously interpreted as longing, nostalgia and resignation.

The architecture and role of ports is

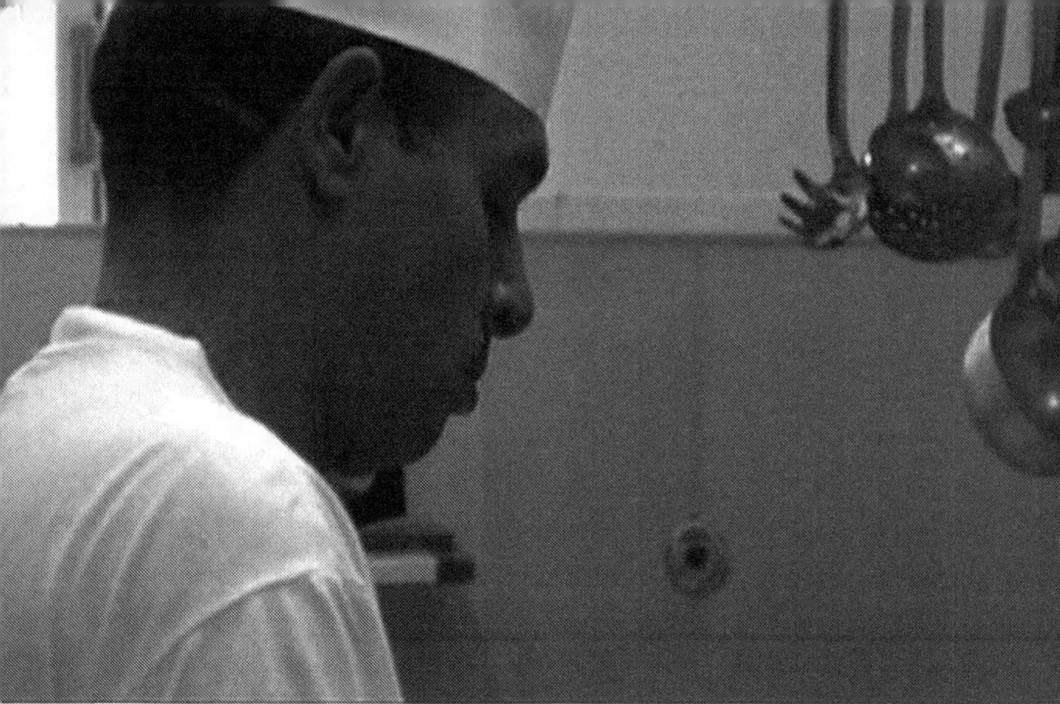

developed in two further films. Charles Heller's documentary, made on a field trip with Ursula Biemann and part of the Maghreb Connection screening programme curated by her, makes a case study of the new port zone east of Tangier, an ironically named 'Free Zone' cut off from its surrounding area by heavy policing and fortress-like planning design, while paranoid clandestines hide in the nearby hills under constant threat of exposure. As Tom Trevor points out in his catalogue introduction, these new peripheral docks, built in the interests of multinational corporations and globalised trade, are increasingly disassociated from the cultural life of the cities on which they once depended. However, it is instructive to be reminded by Paul Gilroy, in his essay 'Offshore Humanism', that off-shore interests have long determined port infrastructure: the fear of theft at

London's West India dock prompted the establishment of the city's first police force.

Raphael Cuomo and Maria Iorio have set their film on the barren Sicilian island of Lampedusa, the southernmost tip of Europe – closer to Africa than Italy. *Sudeuropa* (2006) explores the increased pressures of migration on Europe's newly fortified outer rim, challenging the view that southern European countries unequivocally want to keep migrants out. A helicopter circles the island's cliffs, presenting at once an exaggeratedly nostalgic vision of a relatively unspoilt, rugged corner of Europe and the difficulty in patrolling its circumference against the daily clandestine arrivals the authorities desperately try to conceal from the tourists. Yet while the police bemoan the lack of European funding needed to keep up the constant vigil, the film slyly

   Image: Still from Sudeuropa, Raphael Cuomo & Maria Iorio, 2006 exposes an unspoken paradox. Clips of successful migrants working behind the scenes of the hospitality industry confirm the island's hypocritical reliance on Africans to support its main economy: tourism.

Other artists in the exhibition have used the very materials of their work to express this precarious relationship between the visible and invisible, and the related dichotomy between permanence and ephemerality. Meschac Gaba has created an architectural model of a fantasy port city – squeezing in iconic buildings from around the globe, such as the Eiffel Tower, the Gherkin and the Taj Mahal, in among clusters of generic warehouses, factories and bridges. Built entirely from sugar, *Sweetness* (2006) hovers like a mirage: as seductive as the Hansel and Gretel fairy tale. But behind its innocent, pure white façade, sugar conceals a darker history of slavery and exploitation of first the colonies and now ex-colonial, developing countries. If sugar is associated with decadence and decay, William Pope. L's installation, *The Polis or the Garden or Human Nature in Question* (2006) literally enacts the process of entropy. Industrial shelves support tens of onions, some of which have sprouted, others rotted, sometimes falling to the ground to stew in sticky puddles. Painted black and white, these organic lottery balls suggest the random mix of natural and artificial elements involved in our human fate.

With two screens displaying banal

Biemann is sensitive to the moral dilemma in making visible those who strive to remain invisible

shots of contemporary Britain, West Africa and the southern states of America, Mary Evans' *Blighty, Guinea, Dixie* (2007) looks suitably benign at the back of the Arnolfini's reading room, impressively stocked with photocopied articles from the *Economist* and specialist magazines, print-outs from the internet and a library of books from the now-mandatory *Empire* to volumes on Bristol's slave trade. A telescope standing in front of one screen invites viewers to inspect the grand exterior of a restored American plantation house; but rather than the expected close-up, the viewer is offered a kaleidoscopic spectacle of seemingly unrelated imagery: basket-weaving, a horse in a pasture, the changing of the guard. Gradually, as with all patterns, the brain tries to find links between these three axes of the Atlantic slave trade; Evans again obliquely hints at the history that lies hidden behind the

Jennifer Thatcher

Port City is deeply cynical: freedom is still contingent on the lack of freedom of others

superficial screen of daily images. It's a tenuous exercise but oddly gripping.

There is nothing subtle, on the other hand, about the style of Erik van Lieshout's hypnotic video, *Lariam* (2001) booming out over all the first-floor installations. Ever the Shakespearean fool, van Lieshout here presents a pastiche of a music-video, in which he and a friend, dressed in the decidedly uncool Dutch uniform of shorts and flipflops, travel to Ghana to make a rap song – in Dutch – about the anti-malarial drug Lariam. A scaled-up, scrappy version of the Roche-branded packaging forms the cinematheque for the film. Following a quick lesson in rap technique with a local guru, the video leads to the surreal climax in which an excited crowd of locals, jumping up and punching the air, join in the chorus – Lariam!

The film itself provides little context for the venture: like the locals we are given no translation of the lyrics – which the catalogue later reveals to be 'Instances of suicide have been communicated, but a link with Lariam could not be demonstrated'. But the strength of this video, like all Lieshout's work, is in the odd combination of absurdity and earnestness: a European

geek retracing the roots of rap in a former colony apparently to celebrate a Western drug whose side-effects include depression so severe it has been linked with torture, and whose expense renders it inaccessible to all but luxury travellers. Yet what more appropriate metaphors might there be to raise awareness of a dubious drug with side-effects potentially more dangerous than the symptoms it is supposed to inhibit?

After the epic African journeys that form the backbone of the exhibition's narrative, the British-based works seemed somewhat trivial. Even Melanie Jackson's elaborate pop-up diorama of the recent wrecking of MSC Napoli on Devon's Branscombe beach looked quaintly *Famous Five* – an impression reinforced by anti-climactic testimonies from bemused locals, rogue scavengers and the sleepy village police. The title of the piece, *The Undesirables* (2007) might equally refer to the pesky looters or indeed the mostly worthless or niche-interest bounty that included proportionally more low-value goods (flip-flops, shampoo and dog food) than the prized motorbikes and bottles of vodka. Indeed, if this piece has any resonance outside its local context, it is in bringing to light the unexpectedness of the goods: containerisation has produced a perverse scenario where a ship's contents – which may include a group of clandestines – is a mystery even to those who transport and unload it. More poignantly, Sarat Maharaj's brief account of the drowned Chinese cockle pickers at Morecambe Bay, reproduced in the catalogue only, movingly describes the very 21st century vulnerability of these illegal workers, some of whom had been able to use their mobiles to make a farewell call home to south China, but, with insufficient English and a desperate fear of being deported, not to call for help locally.

Perhaps fittingly, many of the Bristol-specific works in this leg of the exhibition, mostly commissioned by Milanese curator Claudia Zanfi, were taking place outside the gallery, including an ongoing project by Maria Thereza Alvez to grow seeds unwittingly left by the slave ships along with their discarded ballast – materials such as pebbles used to balance uneven cargo. Nonetheless, there was enough to see at the Arnolfini not to feel cheated as a non-local visitor; with a rolling programme of live art and cinema, there was enough material to make several visits. However, it is difficult to evaluate whether Port City will encourage Bristolians, and later citizens of the other cities on the tour, to review their own upmarket waterfront regeneration – including the Arnolfini – in the context of the city's

role in the Atlantic slave trade.

Port City coincides with the 200th anniversary of the parliamentary abolition of slavery in Britain. The selection of works clearly suggests that the exhibition is not a celebration but rather an uncomfortable reminder that the colonial interests that produced slavery in the first instance continue to reverberate in its contemporary manifestations – whether the cockle pickers or people-traffickers. In this, Port City is deeply cynical: freedom is still contingent on the lack of freedom of others. And if the art here might well succeed in rendering the invisible visible, in fracturing the monoculture of the press, it too often fails in another important function: as a space to imagine, and thus sow the seeds of change, for a more positive vision of human relations.

Info

Port City: On Mobility and Exchange, Arnolfini, Bristol, 15 September - 11 November 2007, then touring to John Hansard Gallery, Southampton; A Foundation, and Bluecoat Art Centre, Liverpool. http://www.arnolfini.org.uk/whatson/exhibition.php?id=35

Jennifer Thatcher <jen.thatcher@totalise.co.uk> is co-Director of Talks at the ICA, and a freelance writer

Contagion,
Capture &
Critique

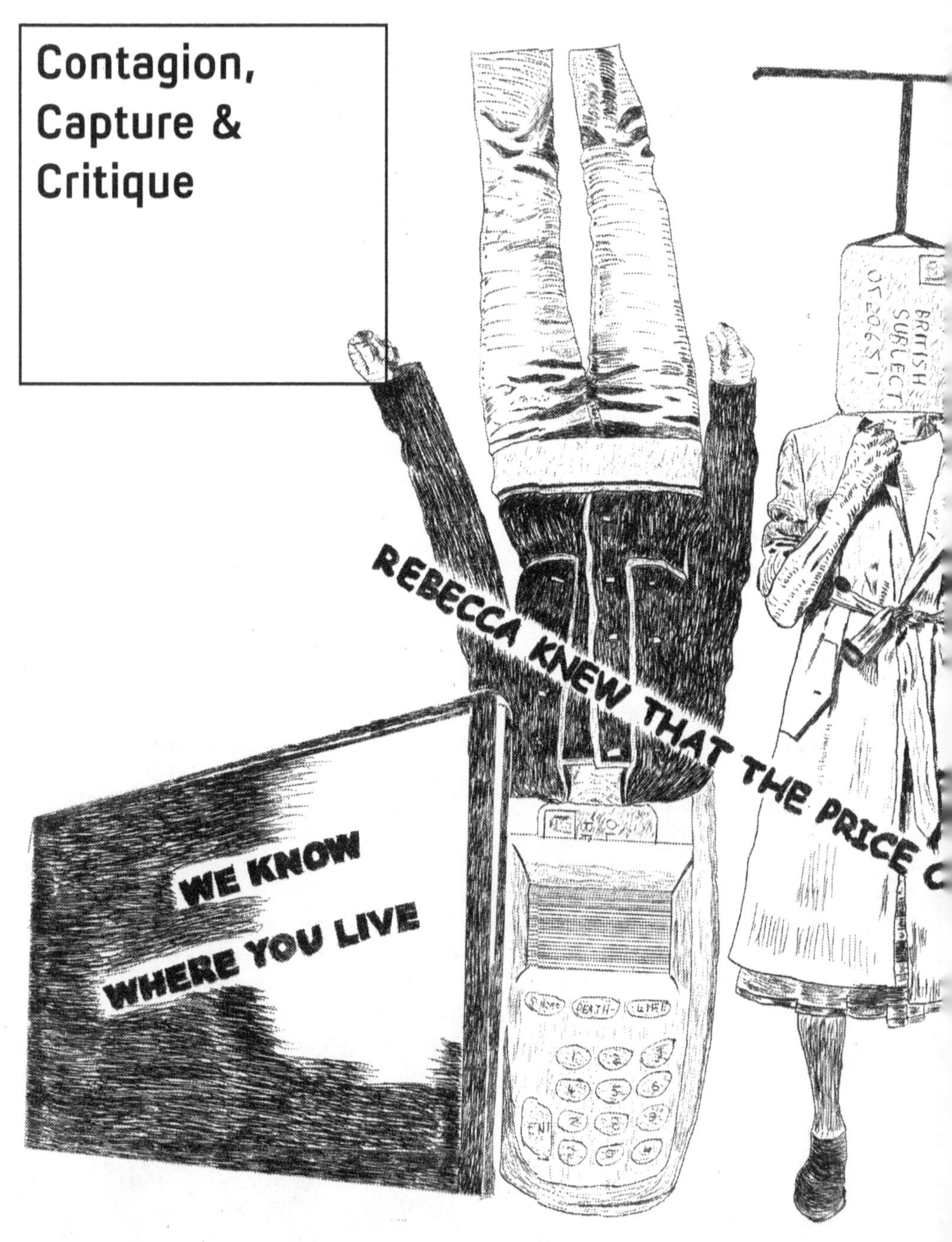

REBECCA KNEW THAT THE PRICE O
WE KNOW
WHERE YOU LIVE
BRITISH
SUBJECT
OF 2065

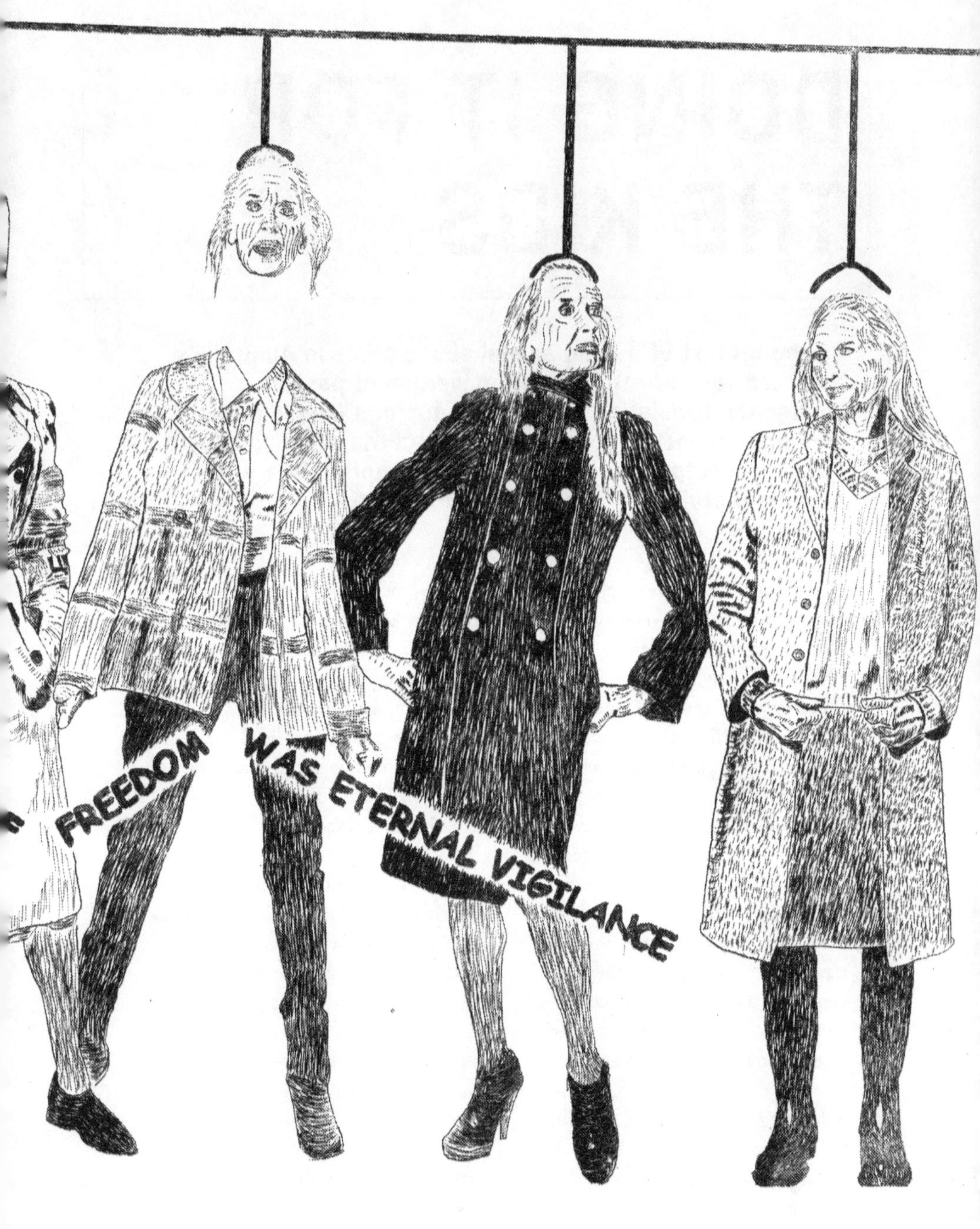
FREEDOM WAS ETERNAL VIGILANCE

DOING IT FOR THE KIDS

On the pretext of a child sexual abuse crisis in Australia's Northern Territory the Howard government passed emergency legislation and prepared a land invasion of aboriginal areas by police, doctors and the army. **Elizabeth Povinelli** locates this latest state of exception in a wider neoliberal project to impose work and austerity

In July 2007 I was living in a small remote aboriginal community called Bulgul, on the coast of Anson Bay, Northern Territory, with a group of aboriginal men, women and children. Most of them were living in tents. These people had been driven out of their homes in another indigenous community called Belyuen located about 300 kilometres from Bulgul. Wielding axes, chainsaws, pickets, and rocks, other members of the community chased them into the scrub on 15 March. Then they ransacked their houses and stole their goods. Initially no one was charged. The police investigation seemed minimal at best. Without any prospect of housing in Darwin, and not wishing to live as part of the urban poor, these exiled people had been promised housing at Bulgul where they could live on land that belonged to their pre-colonial ancestors. Under Australian property law this land is currently defined as 'aboriginal freehold'.[1] Months later they are still living in tents, hauling water and firewood, while, just kilometres away, non-aboriginal people live in houses on aboriginal freehold.

The rainy season begins in November, then the monsoons arrive in December. Members of the federal and Territory government who want these families to go back to Belyuen can count on the weather to push them there. Already in July quite a few of these people had given up and gone to various severely overcrowded indigenous town camps in Darwin. These men and women had job skills in education, construction, and power and water management. In short, they were the kind of indigenous person that the government, given the appalling

Images and text box by Benedict Seymour

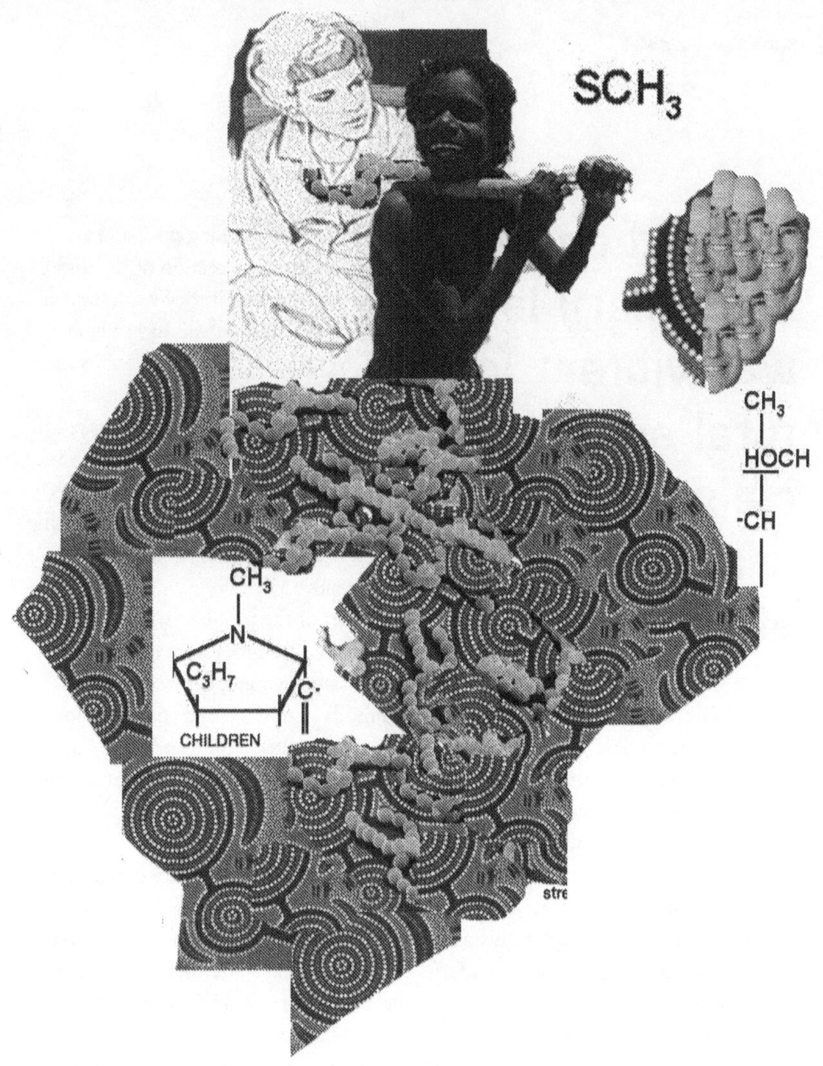

statistics on aboriginal health, employment, and education, would be interested in supporting. But the federal and Territory government continue to pressure the people living at Bulgul to return to Belyuen. They refuse to go, because they believe that if they return they will suffer either violent death or a corrosive life. Why do representatives of State governments and agencies want these people to take this risk?

Bad Timing

Citizens within liberal democracies like Australia tell a certain story about themselves. It is a story about time. In this story, modern time broke with pre-modern time. The progressive time of history replaced the cyclical time of tradition, seasons, mythology, kingship, and tribalism. Modern time cut the circle of cyclical time and made it a

Howard agreed customary law was vibrant in rural areas, but claimed that it sanctions child abuse

straight line. For some this straight line points to a perfectible future. For others this line is going forward but to no particular future, perfect or otherwise. Most critical theorists acknowledge that our experience of time and space can vary under different conditions of state and capital. David Harvey, for instance, famously described the compression of space and time in postfordist capitalism.[2] Harvey notes that how we think about the time horizon affects the kinds of decisions we make. Not everyone can take advantage of the long term or the here and now in the same way. For those able to invest heavily in the financial markets, the here and now can produce massive profits as new communication technology and sophisticated financial instruments allow for near instantaneous trading and profit taking. For most people, the ideology of the market continues to be oriented to a generational future

horizon. The working poor and an increasingly large section of the middle class are told that if they work hard and save, their children will have a better life. My friends at Bulgul would seem to be an excellent example of this ideology of the future. They worked to raise their children's and their own life prospects even as they maintained hunting skills. It might seem surprising then that the State did not invest in their move.

Part of the problem was bad timing. Every so often this story of modern time is suspended. State and public pundits announce that society is now in an extraordinary time and state - a time of emergency and a state of exception - in which the progressive story of historical unfolding must be interrupted. The ordinary organisation of social life has been disrupted or cannot go on as it has been going on. So severe and so devastating have the problems of social life become that radical actions must be taken, rights restricted, new experiments in living begun. We must do something dramatic, here and now, or there will be no future, no there, no then. Unaware of the specific events at Belyuen and Bulgul, but seemingly aware of the general condition of violence in indigenous communities, on 21 June the Prime Minister John Howard announced

a national emergency in relation to the abuse of children in indigenous communities in the Northern Territory.

The politics of cultural recognition (the Australian strain of 'multiculturalism') had massively failed aboriginal people, he declared. Aboriginal people were as badly off in terms of their health, education, employment, and life expectancy as they had ever been. Further, on the basis of customary rights which allow senior indigenous men to claim pre-adolescent girls as their wives, older aboriginal men were supposedly raping their children.

In the name of this national emergency, Howard's government assumed broad and unprecedented powers over indigenous affairs in the Northern Territory including indigenous welfare, education, land tenure, and health. The sweetener was the promise of millions of dollars for indigenous health, education, and employment training. The federal government would send 'business managers' to take control of all Commonwealth programmes in indigenous town camps and rural communities with powers to control and direct all indigenous programmes and their assets. One of the first actions of these business managers would be to shift indigenous workers from the Community Development Employment Programme (CDEP) to welfare.

Such a shift from work to welfare was necessary because the federal government wished to control the wealth and spending of indigenous people in remote communities and town camps. Once all indigenous people were placed on welfare all welfare payments could be tied to school attendance and other behavioural indices; furthermore, 50 percent of payments would be allocated for spending in selected stores where they could only be used for the purchase of food and clothing. Aboriginal citizens would be banned from purchasing alcohol and pornography. Speaking to Leon Compton on Darwin ABC radio on 23 July, Minister for Families, Community Services and Indigenous Affairs, Mal Brough, made the link between welfare and social control explicit:

> Compton: Are you saying that money from CDEP is the problem in child sexual abuse and alcoholism and violence?

> Brough: Absolutely, there is no doubt that there is a contributing factor beyond the CDEP payments and because for all intents and purposes they are a welfare payment – it is the cash that is being used to buy the drugs and alcohol that have caused so many ... so much of the pain for these children. There is just no doubt about that.[3]

In addition to the paternalistic control

NEOLIBERAL DREAMTIME [http://wakipedia.org/wiki/Dreamtime]

Neoliberals believe in two forms of time. Two parallel streams of law. One is the daily objective legality ... The other is an infinite juridical cycle called the "dreamtime", more real than legality itself. Whatever happens in the dreamtime establishes the values, prices, and wage relations of Neoliberal society.

According to Neoliberal culture, the dreamtime is the time of surplus value creation and productivity. In this 'everywhen', a time outside of time, allegations of sexual abuse are used to create a notimetothink and a justintime in which work is indistinguishable from life. Everything is true and nothing is permitted.

THE LIVING LORD

The lord of this special time is called by his ancient name, The Bald Serpent. He controls the supply of money and penicillin and rules by panic, poverty and sores.

In the Neoliberal world view, every event leaves a record in the land. Everything in the natural world is a result of the actions of the archetypal beings, beings whose actions created the world. Thus they get the real estate when the evil paedofolk are driven out.

SAVE THE CHILDREN (THEY MAY COME IN HANDY)

For Neoliberals, little children are sacred, accordingly they may be killed slowly with alcohol and shit work but not sacrificed instantaneously. Many 'Neos' believe that little children are full of untapped surplus value.

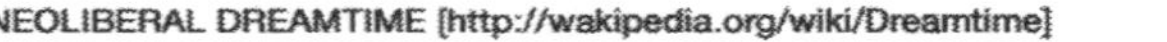

of indigenous income, the federal government proposed that medical volunteers be flown to remote communities to conduct compulsory health checks on all children under the age of 16, focusing on physical and sexual abuse. Military police would be sent to remote communities to control violence and protect health workers. The federal government would take over aboriginal lease lands in townships such as Alice Springs, Katherine, and Pine Creek for five years. Although this represents about one percent of aboriginal land in the Northern Territory it represents nearly all of aboriginal land near white cities.

Sacred Lives

Howard's announcement came in the wake of 'Little Children are Sacred', a report from the Northern Territory Board of Inquiry into the Protection of Aboriginal Children from Sex Abuse.[4] 'Little Children are Sacred' reported an 'epidemic of child sexual abuse' in remote aboriginal communities. It blamed this epidemic on cultural and economic isolation, boredom, substance abuse, and a general lack of hope among the indigenous, young and old. The report contained graphic descriptions of sexual abuse but did not quantify its frequency. Sexual abuse of children was simultaneously everywhere and nowhere. The report did discuss sexual traffic between white men and black women in and around the major towns, rural communities, and remote camps, its historical relation to colonialism and indigenous poverty. It also foregrounded several myths about indigenous sexual abuse including the claim that aboriginal men are the only offenders, that aboriginal law is responsible for sexual abuse, and that aboriginal culture accounts for its low reportage.

However, the report also emphasised - drawing on statistics gathered in indigenous contexts - that most child sexual abuse is committed by a family member or close friend.[5] And when the report circulated in the national press, it was this point — the abuse of children by their family based on traditional marriage laws — that received almost total attention. Conservative commentators rushed to claim their pyrrhic victory, indicting supporters of multiculturalism for their naive understanding of aboriginal customs. National media promoted the pro-market vision of the indigenous activist Noel Pearson.

Although Howard pegged his declaration of emergency to the release of the 'Little Children are Sacred' report, he did not restrict himself to its recommendations. Instead he endorsed minister for Indigenous Affairs Mal Brough's long standing call for a move beyond the politics of recognition and reconciliation with indigenous people to an enterprise approach to indigenous affairs. Indigenous people needed to stop worrying about their culture, move out of rural regions, and accept whatever jobs they could get in the cities. By September, the Howard government, which controls the federal parliament, had passed the Northern Territory National Emergency Response Act, 2007. The Act gave the federal government sweeping powers over indigenous land tenure, welfare, alcohol consumption, and education. Dumbfounded by the legislation, one of the authors of the 'Children are Sacred' report, Patricia Anderson, said that there was no relation between the report and the emergency powers claimed by the government.

Even as the state powers that Howard claimed to need to put these programmes in place became law, the actual programmes — immediate suspension of alcohol sales, deployment of the military into remote communities, mandatory sexual examinations, massive investment in policing, education, and medical care - were immediately scaled back because of constitutional problems including just terms of compensation for the seizure of property and racial discrimination.[6] In order to overcome the problem of racial discrimination, the Northern Territory National Emergency Response Act explicitly exempted the legislation from the Racial Discrimination Act, 1975. The funds promised were slashed and all funds previously allocated to remote indigenous communities frozen.

Indigenous people living in remote communities, or those like my friends who were promised housing in their traditional country, were told to move closer to the cities where infrastructural and service delivery costs were lower, even if their new neighbourhoods would endanger their lives.

Exceptional Times?

Are we living through an exceptional moment? One immediate answer would have to be, no, insofar as today the exception has become the rule. The state of exception, and its tethering to moral panic, is a routinised form of state action. For the philosopher Giorgio Agamben, the state of exception is a constitutional means whereby the state declares the suspension of the ordinary constitutional order. For instance, parliaments can legally declare the suspension of the constitution conferring upon the executive body almost dictatorial power. New state security laws in the US, Britain, and Australia passed after 9/11 and 7/7 suspending habeas corpus and other once almost sacred constitutional protections are examples of this.

To declare a state of exception, a government must present society as on the brink of collapse; political life must be threatened to such an extent that people can be killed with impunity. States of exception do not necessarily depend on actual war being waged against a nation state. Moral panics, and sexual panics in particular, have been repeatedly deployed to create the conditions for states of emergency.

There is nothing exceptional about declaring a state of emergency, indeed the Howard government is prone to do so in the lead up to national elections. Howard's state of emergency in the Northern Territory effectively announced the arrival of the election cycle. In the lead up to the 2001 election Howard claimed that asylum seekers aboard the Tampa, a Norwegian cargo ship in distress off the coast of Indonesia, deliberately threw their children into the sea in a desperate attempt to be taken to Australia. A Senate select committee found this claim was untrue, and that there was good evidence that Howard knew this at the time. Nevertheless, he was able to mobilise national sentiment against asylum seekers and paint the Labor opposition as week on immigration.

In a searing critique of Howard's latest panic policies, Labor MP Marion Scrymgour referred to the Northern Territory National Emergency Response Act, as 'the black kids' Tampa'. (Scrymgour is the first indigenous woman Minister in any Australian government and is Minister for Family and Community Services, and Environment and Heritage in the Northern Territory government).[7] Mal Brough immediately called for Scrymgour to resign. She refused.

Most aboriginal men and women living in the rural north see Howard's actions as part of a longer history of government mistreatment. They are used to being the locus of social experimentation, the nodal point of national anxiety. They are used to hearing government officials announce rivers of money and infrastructure that subsequently turn into a dirty trickle. They are used to hearing, 'Be patient, the future will be better.'

Hegemonising Speech

Howard's announcement was not merely the first tick of the election clock, however. The state of emergency also allowed the government to dominate the political discussion in a way that critics found difficult to oppose. Agamben has noted that states of emergency allow governments to reduce citizens to 'bare life', stripping them of all political rights. Without political existence, the subject of the exception can be treated as mere flesh. But governments can also use the spectre of bare life to justify states of exception and the domestic social experiments they allow. Howard used the black child, abused by her family and culture, to radically reorganise the play of power between conservatives and progressives inside and outside indigenous communities. The articulatory scheme Howard deployed had three major parts: The children must be saved from a problem that lies within aboriginal communities/being/culture; To do this we must declare a state of exception for indigenous people, pass laws that racially discriminate, suspend property rights, and militarise social life; Anyone who disagrees cares more about their left cultural ideologies and their failed policies than the actual fate of indigenous children.

The hegemonising force of Howard's speech act, and subsequent legislation internally split indigenous activists roughly into supporters of state intervention such as land rights activist and lawyer Noel Pearson, and critics claiming that the Act was a land grab, a new form of paternalism, and the beginning of a second 'Stolen Generation'[8]

However, these critics were continually asked the rhetorical question: 'What about the children?' The charge of sexual abuse could not be dismissed. It had to be answered, countered, and debated. This is why sex panics have been so important during large-scale political and economic transformations. They are the equivalent of screaming 'Fire!' in a movie theatre; no one is going to stop to ask: What's going on here?

Have Australia's multiculturalist politics of recognition failed? And if they have, why? To answer this question we must dwell for a moment on the location of the state

Mal Brough recommended the move to an enterprise approach to indigenous affairs

interventions — rural Australia and indigenous slums bordering Northern Territory townships. The state of exception was declared in rural Australia, even as the government was assuming ownership of aboriginal land in and around towns. The isolation of the towns is considered a key problem which Howard proposed to address by doing away with the permit system – itself one of the pillars of the policy of respect and recognition for the indigenous. Under the permit system, aboriginal land is deemed private, neither belonging to the public nor the state; visitors are legally required to obtain a permit if they want to visit, drive through, or work on aboriginal land.

Now, it is perfectly true that indigenous poverty is stubborn in rural areas. But indigenous poverty, isolation, and racism are pretty bad in urban areas too, as is substance abuse.

Why then the focus on rural Australia, rural communities, rural crisis? Why should indigenous poverty, which has for a long time been considered 'normal', now require emergency measures?

The corporeally corrosive nature of poverty is ordinary. What is necessary is to shake this ordinariness, to make the ordinary nature of life (sores, malnutrition, sanitation, poverty) appear unusual even as it surrounds everyone like air. By characterising the problem as the sexual assault of children in the rural aboriginal world the Howard government was able to link its conservative programme to certain progressive romances of the culturally robust rural aboriginal person. Howard basically agreed that customary law was still vibrant in rural areas, but that this customary law sanctioned child abuse. Focusing on the spectacular issue of abuse the Howard government was able to bracket off, for example, the relationship between indigenous poverty and rural white-owned grocery stores and pubs, that profit from indigenous addiction to alcohol.

Ordinary Poverty and Sores

The motivation and source for the state of exception does not lie within indigenous society, it is rather internal to Australian nationalism, and it is two pronged:

– A general collapse of the multicultural compromise in the wake of 9/11. This includes the specific assault waged by the Howard governments on indigenous organisations, but also the stubborn tenacity of structural poverty; its debilitating work on health, the incoherence of property rights (remember, at Bulgul, a white family with a house on aboriginal land where aboriginal families displaced by violence are living in tents), and the co-dependency of alcoholism in rural economies (white owned shops and black customers). These problems have prevailed for years, deepening with each subsequent generation. Murdoch-owned national daily The Australian's editorial attacks on multiculturalism were correct in one sense: the foundational dream of the last 30-plus years of the self-reparative aboriginal subject, nurtured almost entirely by the image of cultural difference and recognition, has been, if not shattered, then severely battered.[9] Embracing the recognition of the worth of cultural difference has not been the magic ticket to a better life.

– The extension of the neoliberal state into every aspect of social life, thus creating a crisis of responsibility and accountability in dealing with aboriginal emiseration. This crisis allows the government to enact the suspension of ordinary law and to experiment with indigenous life, to racially discriminate, to suspend property rights, and to militarise social life. Take for example the rhetoric of failure that we are now hearing, which began with Howard's assault on the Australian government body, ATSIC, set up in 1990 by Labor Prime Minister Bob Hawke which had formally given Aboriginal Australians and Torres Strait Islanders a voice in the processes of government affecting their lives.[10]

We might ask, what has failed? As we ask, though, we must remember the increasing separation of classes as a neoliberal regime takes hold. For an example of social welfare failure we can take the local policy in many indigenous communities of not treating staphylococcal and streptococcal infections until a person has at least six active infections on their body. There have been several reasons given to me why this policy is in place in poor indigenous communities. One reason given is that health officials have to assess the risk of creating a drug resistant form of staphylococci or streptococci as opposed to the value of clearing a person of infection. Since indigenous persons living in indigenous communities will be constantly re-exposed to staphylococci and streptococci, their bodies should be allowed to fight off the infection until antibiotics are absolutely necessary. This risk analysis might make sense if it were not for the fact that these infections are rarely if ever cultured and

that their treatment has not changed over the course of the last 20 years.

When I first began living in indigenous communities in North Australia 22 years ago, amoxicillin or penicillin would quickly cure the infections I had. Presently, doctors on indigenous communities say that these

Sex panics are the equivalent of screaming 'Fire!' in a movie theatre

drugs continue to do so. Doctors in the US say they don't and prescribe amoxicillin-clav (Augmentin). On amoxicillin-clav my infections recede within a week. On amoxicillin or penicillin they can persist for months and then re-emerge — the same is the case for my indigenous friends in Australia. How much would it cost to culture the various sores infesting indigenous Australians? How much to treat them with the proper antibiotics?

Why aren't we doing this? Why, cost of course. Because as much as we hear that these are extraordinary times, they are also ordinary times, the same time it's always been for the radically poor and black. The bottom line is the bottom line: What kind of life is worth what kind of investment? Such

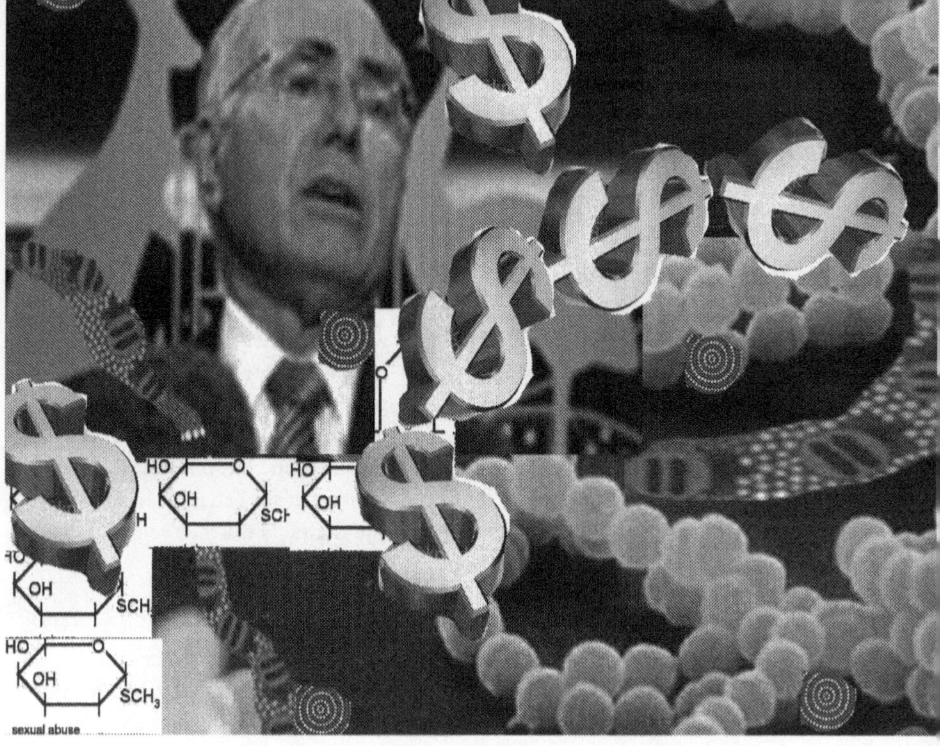

questions need not be asked or answered when we are dreaming of future worlds in which no one has these sores or these life expectancies (even as others are never impeded in their quest to accumulate as much wealth as possible). But the actual cost-benefit analysis occurring is not the balance between the risk of untreated staphylococci or streptococci versus the risk of developing a drug resistant form, but the risk of untreated staphylococci or streptococci within certain populations and the cost of investing in poverty-stricken communities for the short or long term.

The presupposition underlying the treatment of infections in indigenous communities is that the communities themselves will remain fetid. And, within a neoliberal state, any social investment that does not have a clear end — a projectable moment when input values (money, services, care) can be replaced by output value — is not merely economically but morally suspect, no matter what the life-enhancing nature of the investment. Take, for instance, a quite effective programme on rural indigenous communities, The Community Development Employment Project (CDEP). As Jon Altman and M.C. Gray note, CDEP has been described as 'a labor market programme, an alternative income support scheme and a community development scheme', but whatever it is CDEP has raised the personal income of rural indigenous men and women.[11] This basic fact, that a state run social programme increased the quality of life for the most disadvantaged, was judged a failure, however, because it did not project its own end — the movement of indigenous workers out of the programme and into the market. As a result, the Howard government has radically cut back positions available in the programme and increased the reporting requirements for receiving social welfare.

Why isn't the cancellation of this support of life seen as a form of state killing — a form of the death sentence? On the contrary, withdrawing this life support is considered 'a national moral and economic good even though the presence or absence of the CDEP makes little difference to the overall economic vitality of the nation.'

Here, we must remember that Failure, Normality, and Success are not Kantian ideas floating in space but ways of measuring the social world, norms for what is fair or not. Because they are making buckets loads of money, Native Americans able to exploit their sovereignty to establish casinos are considered not to be playing fair. Neoliberal discourse has transformed the organisation of responsibility and accountability. Anything larger than the individual is seen as an impediment to the enterprise subject. Social groups and collectivities as well as long standing federal and state commitments to indigenous social welfare are said to be the cause of poverty. When indigenous people cease to see their social worlds from the perspective of local cultural sense or as related to state-backed social welfare then they will, it is said, emerge from poverty and with this emergence gain the health that all other Australians have.

Once this new regime is in place, we begin to hear once again the reassuring story of modern time, the progressive time of history replacing the cyclical time of tradition and tribalism, etc. But this time round, the measure of the better life is the withdrawal of the state's support for life.

Postscript

On 26 November, the Howard government was soundly defeated in federal elections. In addition to losing the elections, Howard lost his parliamentary seat as did Mal Brough. The new Labor minister for Indigenous Affairs, Jenny Macklin, has, however, refused to condemn the Howard Intervention. Instead she is investigating how the Intervention could be expanded to the other Australian states.

Footnotes

1 The Northern Territory Government describes Aboriginal freehold as 'a type of freehold tenure applying to land granted under the Aboriginal Land Rights Act (NT) 1976. Though simply recorded in the Land Titles Register as "Freehold", land held under Aboriginal freehold title cannot be dealt with as normal freehold as the title vests in the community rather than in individuals.'
http://www.nt.gov.au/lands/lingo.shtml

2 David Harvey, *The Condition of Postmodernity*,

London: Blackwell, 1990, p. 202, but also Part 3.

3
http://blogs.usyd.edu.au/elac/2007/07/ploughing_salt_into_the_ruins_1.html

4
http://www.nt.gov.au/dcm/inquirysaac/pdf/bipacsa_final_report.pdf

5 'Little Children are Sacred', Report of the Northern Territory Board of Inquiry into the Protection of Aboriginal Children from Sexual Abuse, 2007.

6 At the beginning of November 2007, the Bawinanga Aboriginal Corporation and Reggie Wurrdjal, traditional owners of lands on and surrounding the Manigrida Community filed a legal challenge against key elements of the Federal Government's Northern Territory Intervention including unjustly compensated property seizure.

7 Marion Scrymgour, 'Whose National Emergency Caboolture and Kirribili or Milikapiti and Multijulu?' Charles Perkins Oration, 27 October 2007,
http://abc.net.au/rn/awaye/stories/2007/2068672.htm; Jennifer Martiniello, 'Howard's New Tampa – Aboriginal Children Overboard', *Asian Tribune*, 28 July 2007,
http://www.asiantribune.com/index.php?q=node/6307

8 The Stolen Generation (or Stolen Generations) is a term used to describe the Australian Aboriginal and Torres Strait Islander children, usually of mixed descent who were removed from their families, under the rationale of protecting their interests, by Australian government agencies and church missions, under various state acts of parliament, denying the rights of parents and making all Aboriginal children wards of the state, between approximately 1869 and (officially) 1969. The policy typically involved the removal of children into internment camps, orphanages and other institutions.
http://en.wikipedia.org/wiki/Stolen_Generation

9 *The Australian* is published by News Corporation and recent editorials have attacked, on the one hand, Islamic radicals and on the other, the politics of cultural difference.

10 ATSIC, Aboriginal and Torres Strait Islander Commission, was abolished in 2005 after a series of controversies. See
http://en.wikipedia.org/wiki/ATSIC

11 Altman and Gray; see also, Jon Altman 'The "national emergency" and land rights reform: Separating fact from fiction' Centre for Aboriginal Policy Research, *Topical Issue* No. 12, 2007,
http://www.anu.edu,au/caeper

Elizabeth A. Povinelli <ep2122@columbia.edu> is Professor of Anthropology and Gender Studies at Columbia University where she is also Co-Director of the Centre for the Study of Law and Culture. She is the author of numerous books and essays including The Cunning of Recognition (Duke, 2002) and The Empire of Love (Duke, 2006). She has served as a consultant for several indigenous land and native title claims in Australia

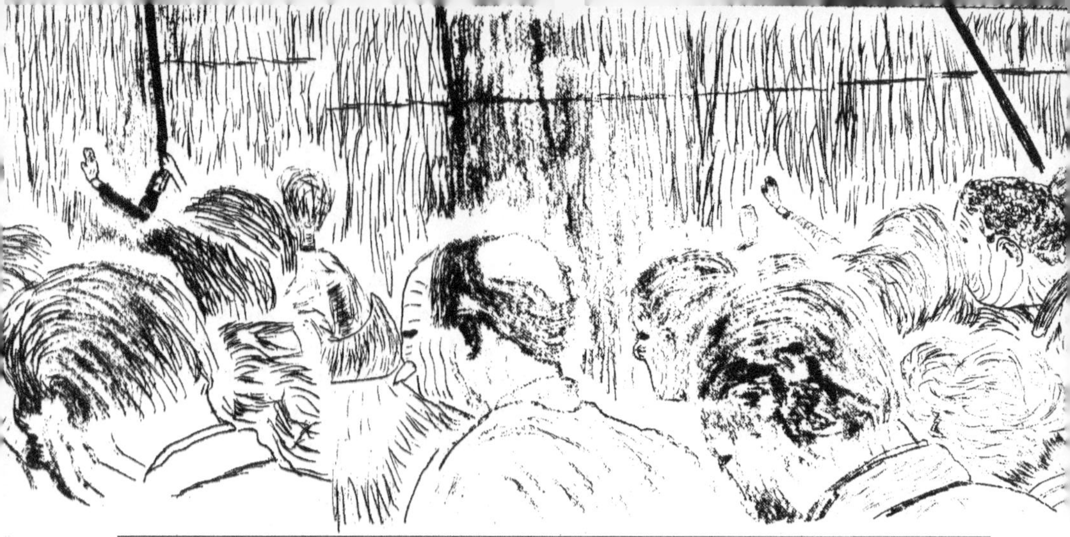

PLAGUE
POLITICS

While bird flu panic has been making a return to the UK mainland this autumn, the promised pandemic has failed to materialise. What does continue to evolve, however, are repressive forms of population management sustained by hypothetical threats of megadeath – writes C. L-Stavrides

D o you remember bird flu? It all seems long past. First there were a few sneezes in the East; then panic swept Europe in the form of wild geese, pheasants and domestic poultry. Wetlands were turned into bio-warfare zones, and eyes were fixed on the skies awaiting The End. So much fear, so much violence, so much state – and yet, the bird flu has been a neglected field of analysis. Perhaps it is the embarrassment of the prophets of doom

that has led them to keep silent as their morbid predictions for a global pandemic failed, or perhaps it is simply the lack of exquisite corpses that has prevented the extraction of some credible form of surplus enjoyment. And yet, even as a failure, or precisely because it is structurally doomed always to fail and thus endure as a threat, avian death persists as 'a shared lie [...] an incomparably more effective bond [...] than the truth'.[1] Thus, today the only available critical analysis of the bird flu is Mike Davis' book, *The Monster at Our Door.*

Unfortunately, the book is full of commonplaces, repeating without critique the media discourse on 'the threat of avian influenza – a plague-in-the-making that the WHO fears could kill as many as 100 million people in the next few years'.[2] Davis presents a narrative that could function as a textbook of asymmetrical threats. The virus is personified and criminalised; it is a thief, a burglar, a hijacker, a pirate, a highwayman, a brigand of genetic material – name it anyway you like, this virus is an entity that violates our most sacred right: property. Of course, our good old bourgeois system has been acutely tuned to that most heinous crime, the problem is that this urthief, this biological substantialisation of theft as-a-thing, has one uniquely lethal property which renders our medico-judicial precautions and restrictions inept – speed: 'the species-jumpers versions are extraordinary shape-shifters that constantly alter the genomes to foil the powerful immune system of human and mammalian hosts. The pandemic threat stems especially from this capacity for ultra-fast evolutionary adaptation.'[3]

What is thus needed in order to counter this deadly effect is, according to Davis, to force the state (and science) to hasten, to awaken, to catch up, so as to fulfil its duty: to provide security against thieves and assassins. But in order to do this, the State must first secure itself by upgrading its containment abilities – or to be more precise, by transforming itself into a mode of containment. The military undertones of this suggestion are evident throughout the book: 'Let me suggest an analogy: during the Second World War, the Allies and Nazis fought a secret high-stakes war over remote weather stations in Greenland, because knowledge of weather-front conditions in east Greenland anticipated western Europe's weather by several days; such intelligence was of incalculable value in planning strategic surprises such as D-Day or the Battle of the Bulge. Likewise, the March 2003 Dutch epidemic proved how crucial veterinary surveillance has become for anticipating human outbreaks. To avoid a catastrophic pandemic surprise, it is urgent to know what is happening on farms months, even years, ahead of any human transmission.'[4]

The question of course is where are these epidemiological Greenland weather front stations to be found? Davis is not reluctant to provide us with the answer. After describing how 'the 1918 flu pandemic dramatically grew in virulence between its initial spring outbreak and the deadly second wave in early fall, so the key variables must have been crowded, often unsanitary conditions with large concentrations of sick victims able to transmit an evolving virus quickly to

All images by Lee Galpin

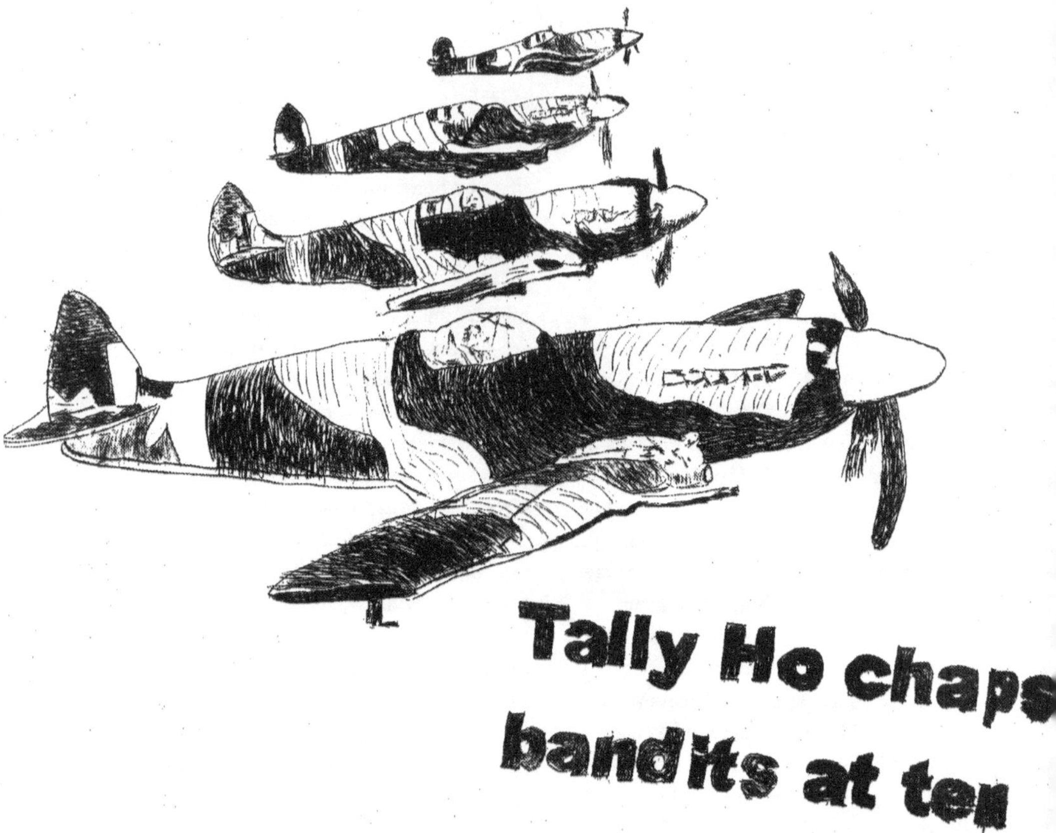

distant location',[5] Davis compares the trenches of Verdun with another 'disease factory', the third world slums: 'while the combustible role of Asia's thousands of slums in the development of a future pandemic has been oddly neglected in the research literature, the great concentrations of urban poverty in Dhaka, Kolkata, Mumbai, and Karachi are presumably like so many lakes of gasoline waiting for the spark of H5N1'.[6] Davis explains: 'the western front of the world's first industrialised war recapitulated much of the disease ecology of the classic Victorian slum –

the locus classicus of most discourse about infectious disease [...] is there any reason to assume that today's bustees, colonia, and shanty towns are any less efficient 'disease factories' than Victorian slums or crowded 1918 army camps?'.[7]

In her paper, 'Not What, but Where?', Mary Sutphen makes the consequences of this discourse quite clear.[8] She explores the reception of germ theories in late 19th century Hong Kong and Calcutta at the time of the bubonic plague outbreak, arguing that 'one reason why many in Calcutta and Hong Kong readily accepted germ theories of plague was because the theories did more than simply describe the aetiology of the disease. Instead they confirmed with 'proof' which could be seen by looking down the tube of a microscope, long-held views on the aetiology of disease.'[9] These were centred around space and class: 'In both cities a faction of physicians and members of the lay public held that the most likely place to find bacilli was in the houses, goods and on the bodies of working-class immigrants, long held to be reservoirs of disease.' Sutphen makes clear that this class-space aetiological conjunction owed much to miasmatic theories of disease and contagion.[10] In the case of Hong Kong, British colonials first noticed the bubonic plague in March 1894. Dismissing theories of rat-related infestation as folk belief, the colonial authorities targeted the poor as the cause of the pestilence, with a special focus on Taipingshan, 'the area where many Chinese labourers lived and where Dr. Ayres, the colonial surgeon, had claimed epidemic disease would erupt'.[11] Isolation of Chinese migrant labourers was the primary method of containment. The problem was acute, but more of an economic than an epidemiological nature: 'one colonial official reported that out of a population of about 200,000 Chinese in 1894 in Hong Kong, 80,000 to 90,000 left the island in May and June. According to the governor, the majority of those who left were labourers who

the virus violates our most sacred right: property

worked as rickshaw drivers, on the docks, or in the sugar refinery. They were men who had left their wives and families behind in China and worked for a period in the colony, sending money back to them […] with the exodus of the Chinese labourers, the colony's trade, manufacturing and commerce ground to a halt.'[12]

Thus, the policy of containment can be clearly seen as a policy of confining the labour force in its place of production legitimised by the discourse of migrant bodies as miasmatic loci of disease. But the confinement of migrant workers in isolation hospitals or boats was only one half of the colonial plan, to be complemented by a second more violent act of urban planning repression. This included the eradication of the living spaces of the migrant workers themselves. 'I need hardly tell you,' commented the governor to the colony's Legislative Council, 'that Taipingshan and a great many streets in Taipingshan will probably be razed to the ground and re-erected on proper sanitary grounds'.[13] The colonial authorities thus proposed

Concentrations of urban poverty are presumably like so many lakes of gasoline waiting for the spark of H5N1

and carried out its program burning down 384 houses in Taipingshan, a plan that pleased both 'those that argued that plague was caused by a specific germ which lurked in Taipingshan and those who held that plague was associated with the filth of the Chinese working-class houses', thus initiating one of the largest urban planning repression schemes in modern history.[14]

The impatient reader will object, yes but aren't all these but some colonial times passed, only vaguely relevant today? The example of Yushu in Qinghai proves otherwise. On 12 July 2005 it was discovered by the Chinese party state that in the farming community of Yushu in Qinghai Province a large number of people had developed acute pneumonia symptoms. The authorities moved into the area and isolated the patients, while forcibly inspecting the surrounding areas. Dr Henry Niman reports that, 'on the 18th July, the decisions was made to quarantine the area. This was aimed at preventing/restricting the movement of people in and out of the area'.[15] These measures however 'led the residents to

"lose control of themselves" and revolt against the authorities, leading to many casualties. To prevent a chain reaction linked to the Tibetan question [...] on the 20th the PLA sent in huge numbers of reinforcements to quell the uprising. At the moment, the extent of the disturbances there is unclear as the area still remains under martial law.'

When martial law was lifted 8 days later, 'natives living further from the area made a trip to the farming community, they discovered that it had 'vanished' together with 3 of its surrounding villages. Only some ruins, blocks from collapsed walls, remained. Apparently, the farms and villages had been flattened and there were signs that they had been razed. It is believed that some inhabitants from those 3 villages were workers in the farm. Around 200 people were estimated to have inhabited or worked in those 3 villages and the farm. Their whereabouts are, as yet, unknown.'

This was a far from isolated incident, not exotic even in the context of China. For as Li Zhang's ethnography makes

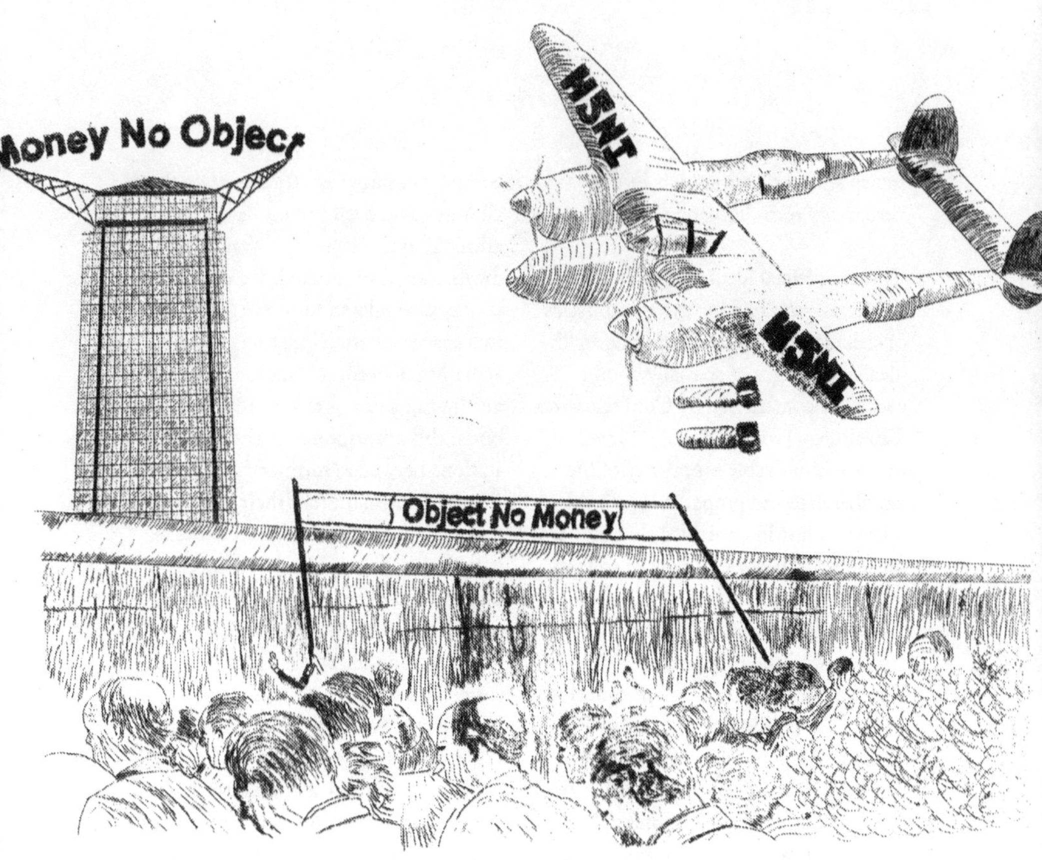

clear, the policy of containment of the migrant population and the demolition of its living spaces features centrally in the official policy of the CCP. In *Strangers in the City*, 2001, Li Zhang tells the story of the largest slum in the history of modern Beijing, Zhejiangcun, home to hundreds of thousands of migrants, which the authorities demolished in late 1995 supposedly in order to restore order and prevent the spread of disease.[16] Li Zhang explains that the Chinese characterisation of the migrant workers as a floating (liudong) population, has two different meanings: 'one is to be lively and unencumbered; the other is to be rootless, unstable, and dangerous. This double meaning opens the image of floaters to multiple interpretations. The dominant discourse tends to invoke and overamplify the negative meanings by emphasising their relationship with related residual terms such as liumin (vagrants, homeless people), liukou (roving bandits), liumang (hooligans), liucuan (to flee), liudu (pernicious influence), liuwang or liufang (exiles), and mangliu (an unregulated flow of people), which is a transposition of the sounds in the derogatory term liumang (hooligans).

Chinese official ideology, Li Zhang claims, is saturated by 'the metaphysics of sedentarism'. This is based upon 'the idealized images of spatially bound social life constructed by Confucius and Taoist texts [which] are often invoked today as a desirable moral way of life' closely related to property, which the migrants, just like the bird flu virus, are presented as lacking or being prone to steal. Employing this discourse the Chinese State criminalised and pathologised the migrants of Zhejiangcu, facilitating their expulsion and the demolition of the area that harboured them. Since then, the policy of the CCP has been to hit hard against the development of slums and to require migrant workers to be preemptively contained within living compounds provided by their employers or industry.

What is thus being problematised here by the medico-military governmentality of the Chinese State, is not so much the migrant workers as a population but as a movement. Similarly it is not the living space of these migrants as topos that concerns the State, but as a transit point. Consequently, it is not surprising that in the discourse on avian flu the chief culprit, the messenger of death, has been none other than migratory birds. By attacking this movement of species across the skies, the biopolitical security complex has in effect tried to state that all unregulated movement is not only criminal, but effectively lethal. This mortification of unregulated movement is of course related to the targeting of two spaces where regulation can be actually achieved: the stations and destinations of migration. In the case of birds, this corresponds to the migration stations between North and South, and the final destination of their big seasonal flight. In the case of workers, it corresponds to state or province borders and other passage points, as well as to the slums where the dispossessed seek their means of survival in a hostile environment.

We can thus conclude that for the CCP, the causal agent of pestilence and collective mortality is migration as a form of subjectivation, not the migrants as a substantial subject: it is the becoming-dirty and becoming-dangerous by means of moving around in space seeking labour, rather than the fact of labour itself. In this way, the CCP can retain its 'socialist' image by not targeting labour per se, while imposing a state of exception on the agents of labour, thus interrupting, mediating and regulating the passage of migrant labour, and confining this labour force in selected and if possible isolated loci near the preferred units of production.This strategy requires both pure violence (such as the razing of unruly slums) and the creation of a regime of fear amongst the non-migrant population – an affective community chez Virilio — based on an imaginary construction of asymmetrical threats.[17] Through these two interlinked biopolitical strategies, both capital and state can secure the reproduction of labour power and guard against any self-organising commotion in its ranks.

Footnotes

1 Slavoj Žižek, *The Metastases of Enjoyment*, London: Verso, 1994.

2 Mike Davis, *The Monster at Our Door; The Global Threat of Avian Flu*, New York: The New Press, 2006, p.4.

3 Ibid p.10.

4 Ibid p.89.

5 Ibid, p.152.

6 Ibid, p.153.

7 Ibid.

8 Mary P. Sutphen, 'Not What but Where? Bubonic Plague and the Reception of Germ Theories in Hong Kong and Calcutta, 1894-1897', *Journal of the History of Medicine and Allied Sciences*, *no.* 52, 1997, pp.81-113.

9 Ibid, p.83-84.

10 Ibid, p.84.

11 Ibid, p.89.

12 Ibid, p.93.

13 Ibid, p.89.

14 Ibid, p.101.

15 All quotes from Henry Niman, 'Avian Flu Pandemic: Chinese Government's Answer "Make Villages Disappear!"', 2005, http://globalsearch.ca/index.php?context=view Article&code=Nim20050804&articleId= 800, see also Henry Niman, 'Chinese Government's Answer To Containing H5N1 & Recombinants - Make Villages Disappear!', 2005, http://www.rense.com/general 67/recomb.htm http://www.rense.com/general67/recomb.htm

16 Li Zhang, *Strangers in the City; Reconfiguration of Space, Power, and Social Networks within China's Floating Population*, Stanford: Stanford University Press, 2001.

17 Paul Virilio, 'Fear and Cold Panic Lead to Collective Inertia', *Eleftherotypia*, 17 January 2006, Athens.

C. L-Stavrides is a PhD student researching biopolitics and the state of exception in China. He publishes the anarchist magazine Flesh Machine in Athens, Greece, and longs for the revolution

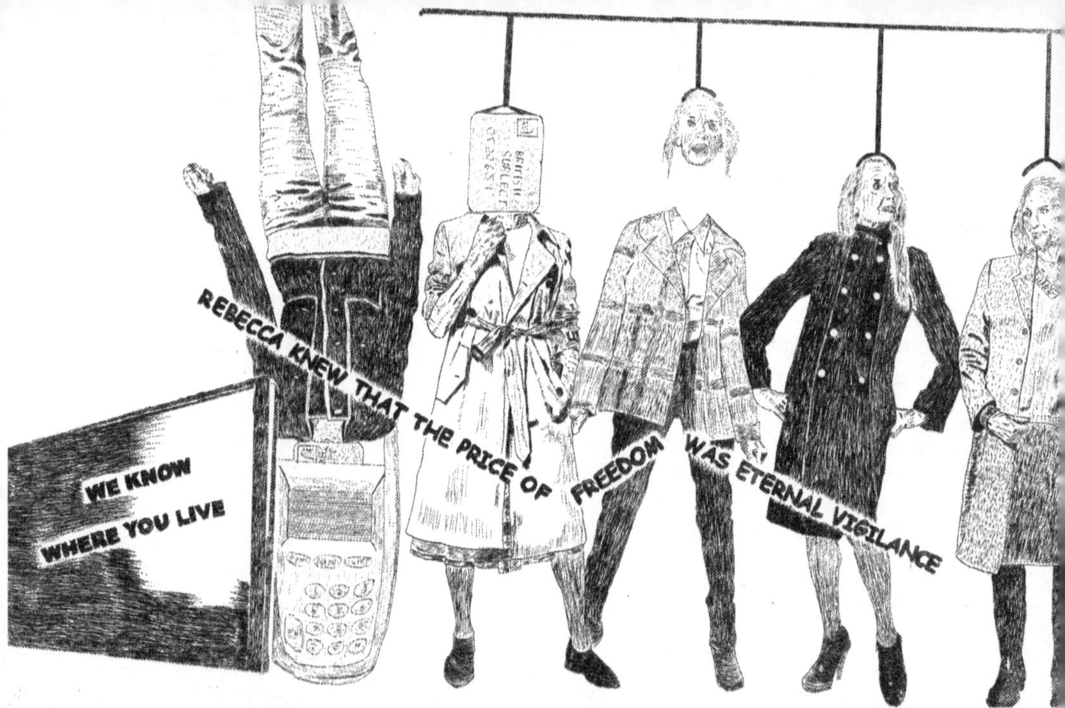

THE SPINE

As HM Revenue & Customs lose 25 million confidential records in the post, the classically wasteful PFI programme to introduce a centralised NHS database slouches on. Total data transparency may be good for corporations and security obsessed governments, but what does it mean for the recipients of 'joined-up care'?, asks <u>Damian Abbott</u>

Just over a week ago, doctors in the north west of the UK became the first to be able to access 'The Spine'.

The Spine is a centralised database of medical records and has already been primed with the details of approximately 50 million patients. Those living in Bolton, some 237,000 people, were recently sent a letter explaining the scheme. Although failure to respond to the letter will be taken as implied consent to the use of their personal data, so far only a small minority have taken the opportunity to opt out.

Although it sounds like a character from Dr. Who, the database programme's moniker was no doubt chosen to evoke an indispensable component of the NHS's target animal. The Spine is publicised on the

Who will the database really benefit?

government's 'Connecting for Health' website as performing five main functions:

– to store personal characteristics of patients, such as demographic information

– to store summarised clinical information which may be important for the patient's future treatment and care, such as allergies, current medications and adverse reactions to drugs

– to ensure the security of systems required to restrict access to the national and local systems [For example, hospital doctors will carry a smartcard as a 'password' to access the database. A 'sealed envelope' system into which patients will be able put their most sensitive information is also under development and will be piloted 'in the long term'.]

– to provide a Secondary Uses Service (SUS), supplying anonymised data for business reports and statistics for research and planning purposes

– to interface with all the local IT systems within the National Programme.[1]

The national programme was created in partnership with British Telecom and a host of often beleaguered sub-contractors including the consultancy Accenture and healthcare software provider, iSoft. Run as a Private Finance Initiative (PFI), it was initially touted as costing just over £2 billion.[2] However, over a decade of development this figure has risen to £12.4 billion. Rumours are now rife that the true final cost will be £20 billion.

A quick review of the history of PFI aka Public Private Partnerships (PPP) makes it clear that value for money has never been the primary motivation for this form of public project. It has always been, first and foremost, a polemical weapon deployed against the very notion of public funding, against the principle of providing services equally to the population through taxation. The first privately financed public project in Britain was a bridge connecting the island of Skye to the Scottish mainland. The governing Conservative Party began seeking contractors in 1989 and construction started in 1992. Estimated to cost £25 million, there were numerous other hidden costs: sweeteners to entice a private consortium of UK and overseas

All images by Lee Galpin

companies into doing the job in the first place; access roads to the bridge which were not part of the deal and were paid for purely from the public purse; decommissioning of the ferry, which would have been the bridge's main competitor for tolls, again at a cost to the public purse. Once the ferry was abandoned, government then had to subsidise bridge tolls for the otherwise marooned islanders, many of whom were enraged enough to carry out a campaign of civil disobedience resulting in about 500 arrests and 130 subsequent convictions, putting pressure on mainland courts. All in all, the hidden costs added up to at least three times that of the publicised cost; the consortium walked away with over £33 million in collected tolls, before the Scottish Parliament bought them out for a further £27 million.

Let's just pause and ask who was on the best side of that deal? It certainly wasn't the taxpayer, but how could it be any other way? PFIs mix the worst of both the private and the public worlds: companies offering to do stuff on the cheap for government bureaucrats with severely limited experience of driving a mutually rewarding bargain. If you were looking for the best bang for your buck – a quality product for the right price, not a fully featured public project from your local Pound Shop – would you really want a civil servant to be your primary negotiator? PPP would probably best be read as standing for Piss Poor Performance, unless your

PPP would be best read as standing for Piss Poor Performance

benchmarks for efficiency were distinctly other than financial.

The NHS' IT programme, however, is hugely ambitious and its size may well ensure a less happy outcome for its corporate partners. The many sub-contractors have had to commit a considerable amount of resources and are consequently shouldering an equally large burden of risk. The contracts were under scrutiny from the beginning, with the National Audit Office beginning an investigation in 2004, at an unusually early stage of the project. The published report in 2006 criticised the speed of progress and lack of consultation with doctors and clinicians. However, the general feeling was that the report itself was lacking, failing to criticise the lack of staff training in the programme.[3] The sub-contractors, too, have been critical of the process, but more because of increased strictures on the deal. Accenture pulled out of its commitments, announcing $450 million in losses due to the delays.

Presumably the contract which they handed over to Computer Sciences Corporation, potentially worth £2 billion, seemed unlikely to live up to its promise given that it stipulated payment in full only on delivery of a fully working system.

iSoft are similarly dubious project partners, although they remain on board. The 'healthcare software solutions' group made a pre-tax loss of £343 million in 2006 on revenues of £210 million, apparently unable to deliver their 'solutions' within any kind of timescale, reasonable or otherwise. In May of this year they announced a board change, kicking out their Chief Technology Officer (with a £250,000 payoff and benefits), then, at the end of October, the company was taken over by IBA Healthcare. The merger has created the largest healthcare IT provider outside of the United States, but whether they too will be swallowed up by their commitments remains to be seen.

Before I go any further I have to declare an interest; I have to say that I'm not writing this article from any kind of objective distance (those who know me will be aware that I rarely do that anyway). I've had Crohn's disease for over twenty years. An inflammatory disease affecting the alimentary canal, and with no known cure, it has positioned me into a regular, almost daily relationship with the NHS for most of my adult life. The many additional symptoms of the disease, affecting peripheral parts of the body, have meant that my sense of self has been fragmented for equally as long, since each new symptom means being shuffled into a new hospital department. Iritis sends me over to the ophthalmic specialist, pyoderma to the skin department, tumours to the oncologist. Drug treatment has been overseen by a 'medical' team, whilst surgical intervention has been the territory of yet another group of professionals. Sometimes they have argued over whose discipline should take precedence, and most of the time it has been as if my body were segmented by a bureaucracy over which I have had little control. And yet I cannot say that it has been an entirely alienating experience. The form of surveillance to which I have been subjected has been of the most intimate and probing kind; my doctors and I have watched parts of my body, even touched parts of my body that my most adventurous partners in love have never even seen, could never even approach. A body composed of nothing but discrete organs, each organ having its own retinue of observers and functionaries. Yes, I feel worshipped, loved even, and have nothing but gratitude for the men and women that have kept me alive, watched over me, and kept me going in one form or another.

So I am, in many ways, the ideal customer for The Spine. It is being sold on the basis that it will provide me with a form of further empowerment:

> Once the NHS CRS [National Health Service Care Records Service] is fully implemented, having each patient's Summary Care Record stored on the Spine will mean that wherever and whenever a patient seeks care from the NHS in England, those treating them will have secure access to summary information to assist with diagnosis and care. This should provide safer, more joined up care.[4]

How many times is the word 'care' repeated in that paragraph? Someone really wants me to know that this is all about 'care'. The Spine offers the fantasy of uniting all the disparate parts of (one more time) my 'care', creating a holistic understanding of my disease. That a digital stitch could create a unitary realm of communication between my disease, my guardians, and ultimately my life, is a very attractive idea. Over the past two decades I have attended most of the hospitals in London (and a few outside of London); sometimes through the gateway of Accident and Emergency, and sometimes by appointment, but rarely however, has communication been a problem. Admittedly my *Britannica*-sized folder of notes has strayed or been delayed on occasion, but thankfully a cross examination of the patient and an assessment of the particular symptoms as presented is what most doctors base

their decisions on. While I can see that, for example, storing x-ray images electronically has many benefits, I am quite capable of informing a doctor of my name, address, and occupation. There must be very few occasions when emergency treatment is dependent on the kind of general, personal information and history that is contained in medical notes. Beyond the sales pitch, I'm sure that most of us, familiar with peer-to-peer music downloads, bit torrents, and the internet generally, were under the impression that a centralised data processing model was a digital anachronism. So whom will the database really benefit? Who will really find the demographic information useful?

The NHS itself is gradually being segmented and territorialised in much the same manner as my own body, but the infection at root of this process is much more easily diagnosed and discerned. Regarding The Spine from much the same perspective as a meningococcal bacterium are the medical corporations with products and services ready to fit the niches being created. As the foreword to the Cooksey Review, a report commissioned by Gordon Brown into 'the best institutional arrangements for the new single fund for health research', explained:

> Combined with the reorganisation of the NHS R&D function to make

The NHS is being segmented and territorialised much as my own body is

it more accessible and transparent for industry, this [the 'Connecting for Health' IT database] opens the door for the UK to excel again in healthcare innovation and service delivery.[5]

The BioIndustry Association has already expressed an interest in using patient information to seek out test subjects, but there is a deeper effect to consider than the prospect of commercial data mining.[6] The modularity indicated by the spinal metaphor is itself the medical industries' preferred commercial model for the NHS. Taken to its logical conclusion modularity means that the NHS will become less a provider of services to the public and more a purchaser of them on the public's behalf. Suddenly, the spinal metaphor becomes less something that makes the medical process directly and instantaneously accessible to me, but more of an obfuscatory mechanism, a middle man for a market that I will not have any direct control over.

The privatisation of health is little more than the consolidation of a triumvirate of power: health, education, and work. While our further education colleges are being exhorted to serve the needs of industry, the privatisation of health serves primarily to make people dependent on work in order to pay the insurance premiums. Everything locks together to make for a docile populace. Should things get out of hand, however, the ability to search a network that provides demographic information, cross-reference that data with an Oyster card trail, and triangulate the signals from a mobile phone, makes CCTV seem quaint.

Much has been made of the security implications of The Spine, primarily regarding the safety of the information contained therein. Apparently, every access to the database will leave its mark on an audit trail, so it is clear who is accessing information and when. This, of course, fails to take into account that tools are used in the most efficient and expedient way for their user, not necessarily in the way in which they were supposed to be used. For instance, there is already considerable evidence that the smart cards that should restrict entry to the

Care Records Service are being shared among NHS staff, making it impossible to track exactly who has accessed the database:

> An NHS trust board has approved the sharing of smartcards – a breach of security under the £12.4bn NHS IT programme because slow login times would otherwise restrict the time of doctors who are busy treating emergency patients.[7]

Ultimately it is impossible to guarantee the security of any database and it will be impossible to guarantee the accuracy of the data that is input. However, identity theft or any other random security breach is really at the lower end of the potential problem. The utility of the Spine to the State is of more concern. '*Rasterfahndung*', an investigative process pioneered by the German Federal Criminal Investigation Office, involves mining networked databases for characteristics that fit a particular profile. First employed in the late '70s during the search for Red Army Faction sympathisers and members, it only resulted in the arrest of Rolf Heißler. Its use re-emerged after the attacks on the World Trade Centre on September 11, 2001. German police started collecting data from universities, registration offices, health insurance companies and Germany's 'Central Foreigners Register'. The profile used was simple: male, aged 18-40, (ex)-student, Islamic religious affiliation, native country or nationality of certain countries with predominantly Islamic populations. Such profiling, whether or not based on a simplistic ethnic, and ultimately racist, assumption erodes basic tenets of justice, adding caveats to the very functional notion of presumed innocence. *Rasterfahndung* is not even a very effective method of investigation, however. When the German Federal Constitutional Court declared the process unconstitutional in April 2006, it hadn't resulted in a single criminal charge for terrorism-related offences being tried. Ineffective, but very tempting to a lazy or authoritarian government. In the case that the government decides that either a 'serious crime' has taken place, or 'national security' is threatened, patient confidentiality conveniently disappears and you may as well start wearing a t-shirt that advertises your number of pregnancies, the number of days you've taken a sickie, and those two empty bottles you've been trying to hide each morning from the boss.

The rise in gun crime has already been taken by the British police as an opportunity to make a moral attack on the ethics of medical confidentiality. *The Guardian* recently quoted a police officer as saying:

> If your ethics are about the preservation of life, then there should be at least the possibility of you telling the authorities if

somebody walks in with a gun or knife wound.[8]

With the State already considering the creation of a national DNA database, a privatised health service means a population reliant on the very insurance companies that would salivate over access to such information. Confidentiality and privacy really isn't a matter of pedantic philosophising. It's becoming a matter of self-defence.

Footnotes

1 The Spine is part of a project called 'The National Programme for Information Technology' which includes the 'Electronic Prescription Service', and a 'Picture Archiving and Communication System', amongst other digital services, http://www.connectingforhealth.nhs.uk/systemsand services/spine/faqs/

2 PFI, http://tinyurl.com/33aq2d See also: Rob Ray, 'The 3 P's – PFI, Private Equity, and Pensions', Mute Vol. 2, Issue 7, http://www.metamute.org/en/The-3-Ps

3 http://news.bbc.co.uk/1/shared/bsp/hi/pdfs/18_08_ 06_nhs_auditreport.pdf

4 http://www.connectingforhealth.nhs.uk/systemsand services/spine/index_html

5 http://www.hm-treasury.gov.uk/independent_reviews/cooksey_revie w/cookseyreview_index.cfm http://www.hm-treasury.gov.uk/media/4/A/pbr06_cooksey_final_re port_636.pdf

6 http://www.bioindustry.org/

7 *Computer Weekly*, http://www.computerweekly.com/blogs/tony_collin s/2007/01/smartcard-sharing-by-an-nhs-tr-1.html

8 Reported by Vikram Dodd, crime correspondent, *The Guardian*, 29 October, 2007.

Damian Abbott <damian@fiercesociology.org> is a co-founder and editor of Inventory and has worked under various pseudonyms on other collective enterprises

TWILIGHT OF THE SWAMPOID

As database profiling of non/citizens grows increasingly pervasive and the dubious promise of 'techno-communism 2.0' haunts the blogosphere, real material differences will continue to sort the technologically 'liberated' from the dataslaves, declares <u>Leutha Blissett</u>

'We' are entering a period when human transactions are being industrialised, even the industrialisation of identity itself. What television did for the imagination, RFID can do for identity. Whereas the bourgeois subject was consolidated as a Sane White Adult Male Propertied Official Identity (SWAMPOID), which realised its tumescence in the transactional act, the purchase, the contract, the transaction from which women, non-Europeans, the insane, children were traditionally excluded, now technology is excavating this quintessence. The industrialisation of the transaction of things will soon overwhelm the SWAMPOID identity. The quantity of RFID transactions will bring about a qualitative change. The SWAMPOID identity has been a myth, even for those who are Sane, White, Adult, Male, and Propertied. For the rest it can only be the realisation of an alienated condition, sought-after as a goal in a 'liberation' which leaves the social conditions in which we live untouched while reproducing the psychological corollaries which haunt the mind of even the most avid critics.

This industrialisation offers the bourgeois imagination the myth of a 'technocratic communism', where dealing with those 'in trade' is handled by nanotechnology. But it simultaneously destroys the natural communism which arises through the human qualities of interaction. The book, like the brick and the bullet, were all parts of the technology which created the bourgeoisie, with their brick-walled towns garlanded with turrets prickled out with muskets, and internally pickled with mass-produced texts – each identical – flying off the printing press. (We trace a direct line from the Calvinists of Antwerp to the book-thumping Bolsheviks of the Third International.) Recently, media art and the fascination with new technologies of avant-gardists and Arts Council alike, has taken on an increasingly similar approach in its lack of critical engagement with form. Artists are content to simply reflect on formal changes. Political engagement is conceptualised as 'activism' which in

What television did for the imagination, RFID can do for identity

effect is just an aesthetisation of politics – a staple of fascist ideology. In order to understand what is going on, and what has gone before, we need to be clear about what we are doing and attack mystical nonsense and confusionist theory as well as overt political reactionary and counter-revolutionary activity. A prime example is Bruce Sterling's concept of 'spime' (space time) in which he defends a glutinated SWAMPOID Identity under the pseudo-innocent term 'we'.

Hypergraphical experiments make it clear that three dimensions require another layer of interpretation. The tactic of the proto-fascists of vorticism was to compress many dimensions worth of information into this one extra-conceptual dimension. In this way they could make statements at a sub-conscious or subliminal level without having to engage in defending their political positions. However, the fourth dimensional viewpoint, whether as an 'intuitive' dimension or as a spatialised dimension of time (intellect), only served to shut down consciousness, precisely at the point when capitalism itself was under threat during the first world war. The intellect was dismissed as bourgeois – rooted in the mechanical universe so beautifully elucidated by Baron Kelvin. Intuition then became fetishised as a mystical device which

rapidly turns in on itself, becoming an essential aid to remote control manipulation through codes and symbols, reaching its apogee as a sequence of 0's and 1's.

Contrary to occult manipulations, communist praxis is in fact open revolutionary praxis. This depends on constantly opening up new dimensions to human activities. Proletarian self-definition and self-defence is part of the seizing of all means of power. This includes the production and consumption of text from (the) letter to (the) number. For while the bourgeoisie claims the ownership and the benefit of resources, ultimately it is the proletariat which has the capacity to create and destroy. Situgraphy is but one praxis which has taken on bourgeois art's manipulations, its de-humanisation and de-dimensional agenda. We aim to elaborate this in a full and conscious way.

Leutha Blissett <leutha@sierraleonelive.com> has been coming to terms with the effects of the Quantum Time Bomb for some little while now. In contemporary circumstances, he finds that the stateless topology of Alexander Grothendieck is proving more fruitful than remaining confined by the precepts of the Situationist International

All images by Lee Galpin

Show Invisibles?

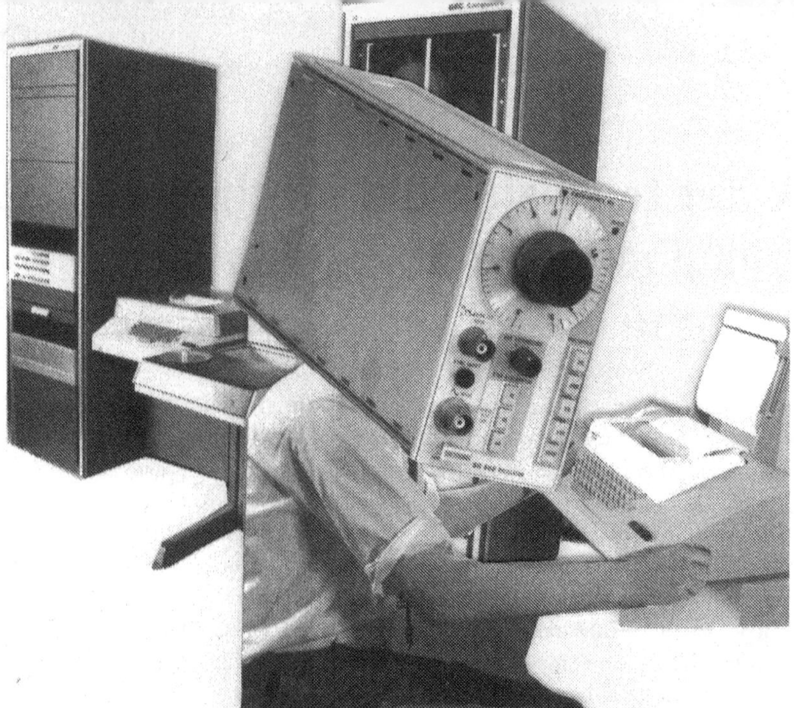

IRONY 2.0

Ironic distance is ambiguous. It grounds both critique and detached resignation to the status quo. What becomes of it in the viral world of web 2.0?, ask <u>Pil and Galia Kollectiv</u>

n 1951, in his film *Traité de Bave et d'Éternité*, Isidore Isou announced:

I believe firstly that the cinema is too rich. It is obese. It has reached its limits, its maximum. With the first movement of widening which it will outline, the cinema will burst! Under the blow of a congestion, this greased pig will tear into a thousand pieces. I announce the destruction of the cinema, the first apocalyptic sign of disjunction, of rupture, of this corpulent and bloated organisation which calls itself film.

This prophecy could be seen as coming to pass with the fragmentation of moving image and cultural production brought about by web 2.0. However, its implications for what we understand to be the relationship between culture and critique far exceed those foreseen by Isou. Much of the critical thinking around web 2.0 has so far focused on issues of authorship and ownership, participation and consumption, the internet as public sphere, communication and community, the alienated labour of the creative industry worker, the commodification of information, opinion and taste. In short, a lot of the writing on the subject adopts a 'strategic' point of view, to use Michel de Certeau's distinction, rather than a 'tactical' one. The goals of this strategic investigation can be diverse: Richard Barbrook champions an 'anarcho dotcommunism'[1] while Manuel Castells describes the 'unseen logic of the meta-network, where value is produced, cultural codes are created and power is decided'.[2] But whether exposing the concealed relationship between institutions and mechanisms of power and control, re-establishing such institutions and mechanisms or seeking alternatives to them online, most readings, stemming from a socio-economic point of view, ultimately rely on an understanding of complex social practices as a superstructure within which differences, hybrid forms and cultural meanings become an undifferentiated morass of exploitation and oppression. In discussing the rise of the virtual, localised uses of networking websites within geographic communities get ignored. Bulletins, blogs, vlogs, comments, photos, mp3s and other forms of media and interaction get reduced to a corporate platform understood purely in terms of technical innovation and monetary value. However, the practices associated with the new platforms for user-generated content referred to as web 2.0 require a more detailed analysis. If we are to see these activities as a truly new field of cultural production, we need to stop applying paradigms borrowed from pre-existing notions of critique. More importantly, in doing so we can begin to address the limitations of this critique more generally and open up a space for new forms of critique to emerge.

One strand of criticism against web 2.0 seems to come from a reactionary position, which sees in the democratisation of knowledge proposed by such sites as Wikipedia a threat to established hierarchies of experts and amateurs. The kind of emergent knowledge produced by users' contribution to editable entries is perceived as a 'dumbing down' of culture. In *The Cult Of The Amateur: How Blogs, Wikis, Social Networking, and the Digital World are Assaulting our Economy, Culture and Values*, Andrew Keen writes:

> We – those of us who want to know more about the world, those of us who are the consumers of mainstream culture – are being seduced by the empty promise of the 'democratised' media. For the real consequences of the Web 2.0 revolution is less culture, less reliable news, and a chaos of information.[3]

 All images by Pil and Galia Kollectiv **Show Invisibles?**

The idea that online social relations are inauthentic assumes that unmediated relations exist offline

Keen binds this anti-democratic sentiment to a defense of copyright against the ease of online appropriation that goes hand in hand with sites like YouTube. These issues, the ownership of truth and of intellectual property, are clearly related in their attachment to an order that is being undermined by a new mass culture. But what is interesting is what this critique shares with its more left-leaning allies, who would otherwise support the weakening of the same mechanisms of control that Keen wants to strengthen.

To the twin conservative critiques raised by Keen, more progressive critics add two more complaints: web 2.0 posits a regime of simulation in which spectacularised human relations supplant 'real' lived ones; moreover, those participating in these relations unwittingly contribute their immaterial labour to a capitalist market in which work and leisure are no longer differentiated. In the first instance, real friends are replaced with Friendsters, MySpace contacts or Facebook friends:

> Sit someone at a computer screen and let it sink in that they are fully, definitively alone; then watch what happens. They will reach out for other people; but only part of the way. They will have 'friends', which are not the same thing as friends, and a lively online life, which is not the same thing as a social life; they will feel more connected, but they will be just as alone.[4]

This neo-platonic idea that mediated social relations are somehow inauthentic, like the idea that truth is corrupted online, assumes that 'real' truth, unmediated relations and authentic, singular selfhood exist offline. For Žižek, however, if we concede that the self revealed online is possibly more real, inverting the dichotomy, the consequences for society are even more dire:

> The fact that I perceive my virtual self-image as mere play thus allows me to suspend the usual hindrances which prevent me from realising my 'dark half' in real life. My electronic id is given wing. And the same goes for my partners in cyberspace communication. I can never be sure who they are: are they really the way they describe themselves, is there a 'real' person at all behind a screen persona, is the screen persona a

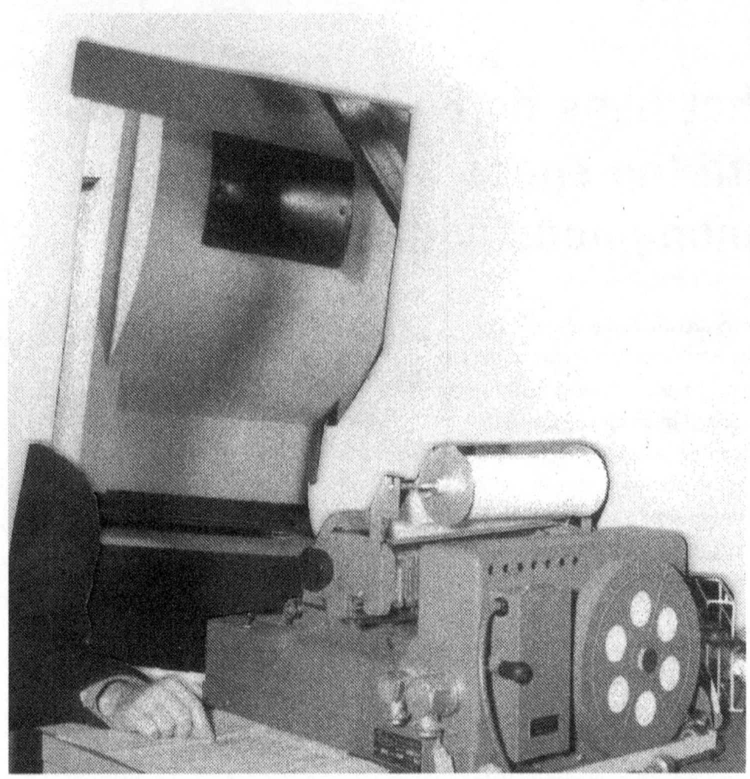

mask for a multiplicity of people, or am I simply dealing with a digitised entity which does not stand for any 'real' person? 'Interface' means precisely that my relationship to the other is never face-to-face, that it is always mediated by digital machinery.[5]

Žižek pulls the rug under the hierarchy that locates the real offline, but retains a hierarchical construction within his scheme, derived as it is from the psychoanalytical distinction between ego and id.

This critique of the confusion arising from the interfacing of technology and sociality is mirrored in the second complaint around the dissolution of the boundaries of work and leisure online. One not only experiences a new kind of alienation from the self (even if as a heightened, more real than real subjectivity à la Žižek) within this pseudo-community, but also a new kind of alienation from the fruits of one's labour. Postfordist or immaterial labour, which 'produces the informational and cultural content of the commodity',[6] to use Maurizio Lazzarato's terminology, has greatly expanded the creative industry, turning

What films do best is provide us with the space of irony, synonymous with critique

formerly artistic and even political activity into a leading sector of the job market, in a much rehearsed argument summarised by Paolo Virno: '[t]he dividing line between Work and Action, which was always hazy, has now disappeared altogether.'[7] The unwitting or unremunerated culturepreneurs of web 2.0 are thus victims of a false consciousness which, unlike the more traditional Marxian one, doesn't just turn them into passive consumers, but actually exploits their active resistance and creativity to generate profits and appropriate their output. Not only is 'the postindustrial commodity […] the result of a creative process that involves both the producer and the consumer', but,

> immaterial labor produces first and foremost a social relation – it produces not only commodities, but also the capital relation.[8]

Participants in new internet platforms contribute their time and energy in producing videos for YouTube, uploading images to Flickr and making music to fill up MySpace, but above and beyond this what they contribute to the speculative economy generated by

these websites and their accompanying technologies is their communicative skills, their networks of friends within which such content is circulated and manipulated.

The reception of these cultural products therefore becomes an integral part of their production:

> In the first place, as the addressee of the ideological product, the public is a constitutive element of the production process. In the second place, the public is productive by means of the reception that gives the product 'a place in life' (in other words, integrates it into social communication) and allows it to live and evolve. Reception is thus, from this point of view, a creative act and an integrative part of the product.[9]

It is precisely because of the centrality of this activity to the production of content on web 2.0 that much of this criticism, with its focus on a truth to be uncovered about what is really going on, finds itself at an impasse. The challenge to authorship online far exceeds questions of ownership and exploitation, and to address it we need to look at the ways in which not just products but meanings are forged in this context. Jaron Lanier is right to complain about 'the lack of a coherent voice': sites and applications such as YouTube, MySpace TV and Google Video erode the coherence of cinematic work and threaten its status as the most significant product of the culture industry.[10] In an issue devoted to 'distributed aesthetics', contributors to online journal *Fibreculture* have already noted that changes in the form of spectatorship, from the mass audience of the darkened movie theatre to the distributed aloneness of the computer screen have contributed to the emergence of new artistic sensibilities.[11] However, the implications of this transition from film to viral video, or from newspaper to blog, go beyond the aesthetic.

What films do best is provide us with the space of irony which has become synonymous with critique. The cuts, the layering of sound and vision, the limited scope and proportions of the cinematic frame, the always questionable neutrality of the camera, all construct a Swiss cheese arena of negative spaces, each defined by the gaps or holes of knowledge surrounding it. One either reads with the audience against the grain of the Hollywood epic, exposing an obscure level of meaning (something we all know the film doesn't know, to use Žižekian terms) or with the film against the audience (the ignorant passive viewers who 'share' the sadistic fantasy of a

moral distinction between 'good' and 'bad' of the epic, only to 'realise' in the end that they too are being implicated in its violence). For instance, a film like *Top Gun* can be read as a homoerotic narrative, exposing the underlying homoeroticism of macho American militarism (and indeed artist Don Bury has proposed such an interpretation in a video that re-edits the film to underline this). Meanwhile, a film such as *Starship Troopers* itself proposes an ironic relationship to its subject matter, leading the viewer to assume a degree of identification with the 'filmmaker' against the film, or the social scenario it presents of unqualified support for the military. In both cases, a gap opens between what we see and how we interpret it which produces a sense of criticality. Even if we know that the 'authorial' voice is something we construct, we can still seek to find 'unintended' or 'subconscious' meanings within it. This is for instance what psychoanalytical or feminist readings of texts classically do, what Irit Rogoff terms

> the endless cataloguing of the hidden structures, the invisible powers and the numerous offences we have been preoccupied with for so long.[12]

But to do this you need to assume a stable position to argue with or to ironise. This logic of irony in the cinema, the space between 'intention',

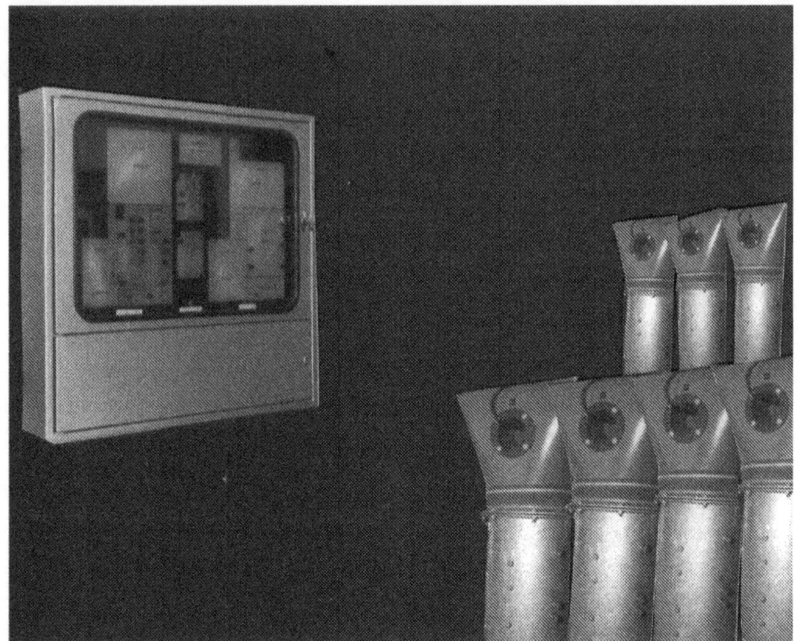

however constructed, and action or surface, becomes nearly impossible when confronted with the viral video of web 2.0. The difference in our relationship to such 'texts' and to more traditional media is between reading 'with' and 'against' the grain and not even seeing any grain. The basic question which the spectator in the cinema asks – 'why is this being shown to me and why am I not permitted to see that?' – loses all relevance in the endless sea of home videos, fragments of obscure music videos, webcam diaries, video-game captures etc. Instead of the artful economising of the cinematic image, we are flooded with the off-the-cuff spontaneity of uploaded amateur media. Because of the viral nature of these websites, questions of originality and authorship become pointless: only after numerous versions of the memorable 'Dramatic Chipmunk' clip (the camera closing in on a terrified looking prairie dog, cast and recast as James Bond or a character in *Kill Bill*) did we stumble upon the original Japanese television show from which the five second clip was edited, and by that point it was no longer an original in any meaningful way, only another variation on the theme. Without a clear authorial voice, ironic subversion makes way for appropriation.

Interpretation, rather than taking a secondary role in deciphering 'true' meanings becomes primary, a fiction on the same level as the 'work' itself. Web 2.0 challenges previous distinctions of private and public, of what one is permitted to see or barred from seeing. Žižek, one of the great masters of dismantling ironic gaps of knowledge in cinematic works, writes that the notion of citizenship under the late communist regimes of Eastern Europe was constituted on an ironic gap between the private, in which one

The challenge to authorship online far exceeds questions of ownership and exploitation

criticised the regime, and the public sphere in which one participated in party functions and rituals, creating a sense of inauthenticity and personal guilt. This actually creates the mechanism of control through guilt that Žižek identifies as a distinctive feature of the late Communist regimes:

> we thus had a regime that actively condoned and relied on the moral bankruptcy of its subjects. This actual shared guilt provides the disavowed foundation of the spectre of the 'objective guilt' evoked by the Communist regime.[13]

We can perhaps compare this observation to the quiet collaboration of the artist in an alienated art market: we all hate the art fair in pub conversations, but agree to participate in them because 'an artist has got to make a living', leaving us with the confused sense of self-betrayal. Web 2.0 makes this conflict between private and public vanish, the pub conversation becomes the business card, blogs proclaim what has traditionally been said behind people's backs. Even *Vogue*'s Nicholas Coleridge remarks in astonishment:

Facebook has altered our concept of privacy. Rich people who loftily decline to list their home in Who's Who are there, complete with specially commissioned photograph.[14]

On Facebook, blogs and forums, what we hide from the world becomes our most visible trait. Gradually, the ironic gap between the social and the professional is closing. Journalists often complain of the cowardly cruelty of users who write comments, or talkbacks, in response to an online article. But isn't this the kind of violent externalisation and dramatisation of opinion that is lacking in an unengaging political arena?

The question that we are presented with is not one of uncovering the hidden system of power relations that is duping us into being exploited. This is not a case of the users being used. Rather, we need to find a new language of critique that takes for granted the possibility that the truth is not out there and doesn't matter anyway, that there is no longer an ironic gap to be narrowed. Just as Walter Benjamin recognised that literature and theatre could no longer form the basis of a critique in the face of cinema, we need to ask what the performances we undertake and are subjected to online require of us politically. We are witnessing exchanges of information in which we may never know what an author might have intended, whether the person who posted the clip or set up the profile was joking or not, and we need to discover a new political praxis that acknowledges this interface as a valid form of communication, regardless of its instrumentalisation within an economic scheme. It is not that subversion can't happen under the noses of Murdoch et al, oblivious to users' manipulation of their spectacular technologies, but that the failed dialectic of subversion and hegemony, in which users don't know what they are doing and end up reinforcing or being co-opted by the system, is annihilated in the post-ironic sphere of web 2.0, where that knowledge is immanent. The moment of truth, or revelation, is no longer the punch line of critique, but the starting point of production. Writing about the role of critique in relation to the digital economy, Tiziana Terranova claims:

> As the spectacular failure of the Italian Autonomy reveals, the purpose of critical theory is not to elaborate strategies that then can be used to direct social change. On the contrary, as the tradition of cultural studies has less explicitly argued, it is about working on what already

exists, on the lines established by a cultural and material activity that is already happening [...] Rather than retracing the holy truths of Marxism on the changing body of late capital, free labor embraces some crucial contradictions without lamenting, celebrating, denying, or synthesizing a complex condition.[15]

We can therefore no longer rely on critique, which we understand as an ironic distance between our enlightened consciousness and those duped by the system, to produce resistance. As Paolo Virno has noted, '[t]he dividing line between Work and Action, which was always hazy, has now disappeared altogether.' Instead of striving to uncouple work and political action, we must turn our gaze to the equivocal action latent within our new regimes of work as leisure.

Footnotes

1 Barbrook uses the heading 'The Net as Really Existing Anarcho-Communism' to discuss an online gift economy transcending the net's military origins and capitalist instrumentalisation. Richard Barbrook, 'The Hi-Tech Gift Economy', *First Monday* Special Issue #3: Internet banking, e-money, and Internet gift economies, December, 2005, http://www.firstmonday.org/issues/issue3_12/barbrook/#author

2 Manuel Castells, *The Rise of the Network Society*, Malden, MA: Blackwell, 2000, p. 508.

3 Andrew Keen, 'The Great Seduction', extract from *The Cult Of The Amateur: How Blogs, Wikis, Social Networking, and the Digital World are Assaulting our Economy, Culture and Values*, New York: Random House, 2007, http://andrewkeen.typepad.com/

4 John Lanchester, 'A bigger bang', *The Guardian*, 4 November 2006, http://www.guardian.co.uk/weekend/srewkeen.typepad.com/

5 Ibid.

6 Slavoj Žižek, 'Is this digital democracy, or a new tyranny of cyberspace?', *The Guardian*, 30 December 2006, http://www.guardian.co.uk/comment/story/0,,1980156,00.html

7 Maurizio Lazzarato, 'Immaterial Labour', 1997, translated by Paul Colilli and Ed Emery, http://www.generation-online.org/c/fcimmateriallabour3.htm [currently offline]

8 Paolo Virno, 'Virtuosity and Revolution', http://www.16beavergroup.org/mtarchive/archives/000941.php

9 Maurizio Lazzarato, op.cit.

10 Ibid.

11 Jaron Lanier, 'Digital Maoism: The Hazards of the New Online Collectivism', Edge, 30 May 2006, http://www.edge.org/3rd_culture/lanier06/lanier06_index.html

12 Lisa Gye, Anna Munster and Ingrid Richardson, [eds.], *Fibreculture*, issue 7, December 2005, http://journal.fibreculture.org/issue7/index.html

13 Irit Rogoff, 'Academy as Potentiality', 18 February 2007, http://summit.kein.org/node/191

14 Slavoj Žižek, *Did Somebody Mention Totalitarianism? Five Interventions in the (Mis)use of a Notion*, London: Verso, 2001, p. 91.

15 Nicholas Coleridge, 'Everybody's At It', *Vogue*, London: Conde Nast, December issue, 2007, p. 138.

Pil and Galia Kollectiv <info@kollectiv.co.uk> are artists, writers and curators. Their film and performance work explores the way utopian discourses operate in the context of creative work and instrumentalised leisure in relation to the paradigms of modernism. They also teach at Goldsmiths College and Hertfordshire University and are the London editors of Art Papers.
http://www.kollectiv.co.uk

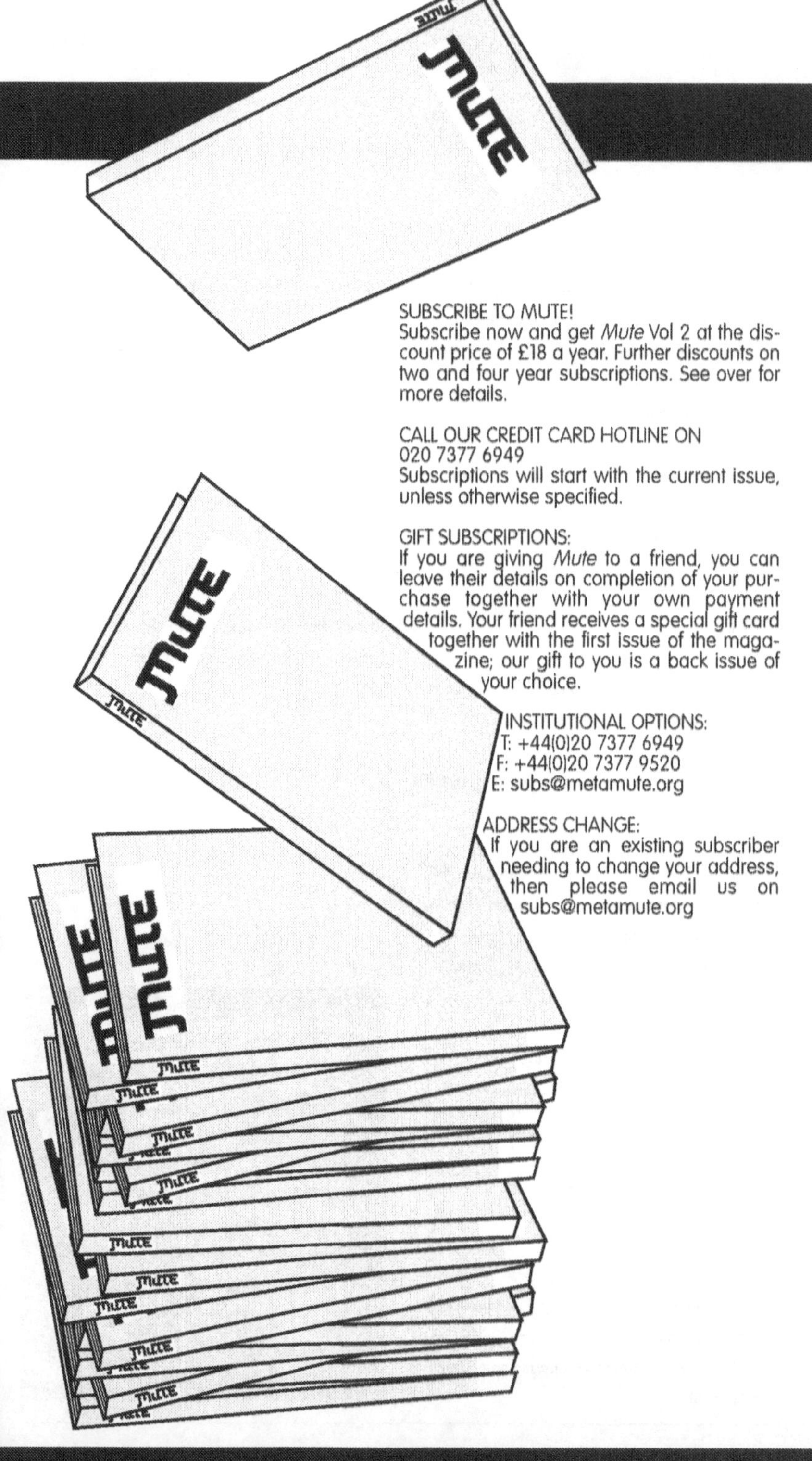

SUBSCRIBE TO MUTE!
Subscribe now and get *Mute* Vol 2 at the discount price of £18 a year. Further discounts on two and four year subscriptions. See over for more details.

CALL OUR CREDIT CARD HOTLINE ON
020 7377 6949
Subscriptions will start with the current issue, unless otherwise specified.

GIFT SUBSCRIPTIONS:
If you are giving *Mute* to a friend, you can leave their details on completion of your purchase together with your own payment details. Your friend receives a special gift card together with the first issue of the magazine; our gift to you is a back issue of your choice.

INSTITUTIONAL OPTIONS:
T: +44(0)20 7377 6949
F: +44(0)20 7377 9520
E: subs@metamute.org

ADDRESS CHANGE:
If you are an existing subscriber needing to change your address, then please email us on subs@metamute.org

go to www.metamute.org/product

subscribe

Subscription Rates:

	individual		institutional/company	
	4 issues (1 year)	8 issues (2 years)	4 issues (1 year)	8 issues (2 years)
uk	£20	£38	£35	£67
eu	€28	€52	€48	€91
usa	$40	$75	$70	$133
other	€34	€60	€54	€102

Please tick the appropriate box.

I wish to pay by cheque/credit card.

- [ ] I enclose a cheque (GBP) made payable to Mute.
- [ ] Please charge my

[ ] Visa [ ] Access [ ] Mastercard [ ] Switch

Card no.

Expiry date   /

[Switch only] Issue number   Start date   /

Signature

name

address

town/city

post code

country

POST TO:
MUTE, Unit 9, The Whitechapel Centre
85 Myrdle St., London E1 1HL, UK

Or call our credit card hotline 020 7377 6949,
Fax 020 7377 9520

Web http://www.metamute.org/product
Email mute@metamute.org

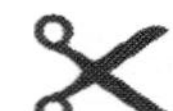